THE TESTIMONY OF BAPTISM

The
TESTIMONY of
BAPTISM

ERROLL HULSE

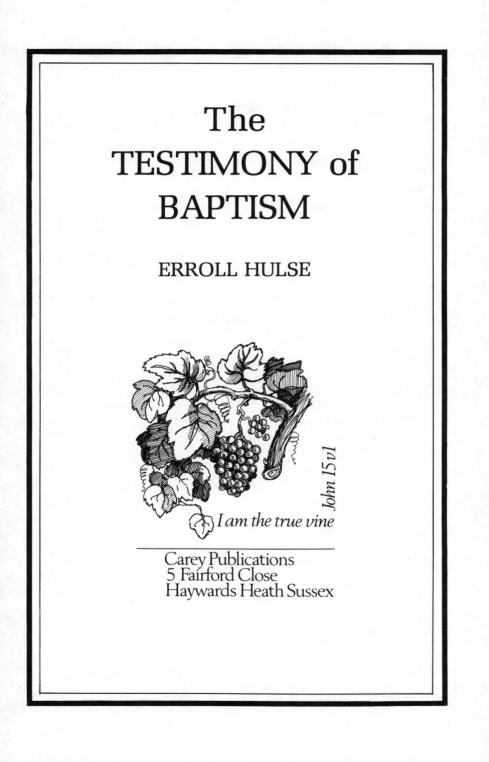

I am the true vine

John 15 v1

Carey Publications
5 Fairford Close
Haywards Heath Sussex

ISBN 085479 0462

First edition 1982

Cover design by
Lawrence Littleton Evans
Illustrations by the author

Printed by Stanley L. Hunt (Printers) Ltd, Rushden, Northamptonshire

Foreword

DR. J. DOUMA who is a tutor at Kampen Seminary in Holland wrote a 36 page treatise with the title *Infant Baptism and Regeneration*[1]. In his exposition he describes the church at Cuckfield in a very generous way. He goes on to explain our difference over infant baptism. On all major doctrines we are in unity. It is not right for this issue to be a source of contention. Our fellowship at Cuckfield with them is rich and mutually advantageous. We desire that it should stay that way. Subsequent to Dr. Douma's treatise several articles on the covenant and baptism were published in the bi-monthly magazine *Reformation Today* (issues 53, 54, 55 and 57). These studies are reproduced as Part 2 of this book. Primarily they are designed to show that Reformed Baptists believe in the covenant of grace with as much consistency as Presbyterians. The only substantial difference is that we stress *both* the unity and diversity of the covenants. We believe that it is their unwillingness to face up to the implications of the radical difference between the Old and the New Covenant (Heb. 8:7ff.) that prevents them from accepting our position.

Dr. Douma attempts to move the whole debate from believers to infants. David Kingdon's book *Children of Abraham*[2] could hardly be more clear. Especially is he lucid in his final chapter, 'Children and Regeneration'. He shows that it is not possible to settle the issue of baptism *there*. The theme or central subject of the New Testament is justification by faith, not infant regeneration. We do not go into all the world to regenerate infants. We go into all the world to preach the Gospel to every creature. Justification is for believers. So is baptism.

Dr. Douma did succeed in exposing our need to be more detailed in the basic issues underlying the practice or ordinance of believers' baptism. Baptists are very poorly equipped as far as expository materials are concerned. Part 1 consisting of 15 chapters attempts to meet this need.

[1] Copies are available from the Christian Bookshop, 15 College Square East, Belfast BT1 6DD, N. Ireland.
[2] Carey Publications. This valuable title is at present out of print. It is hoped that a new edition will be made available.

Acknowledgments

In previous books I have not acknowledged help received out of concern that I might embarrass friends whose views would not be identical with the exposition. As we gain in experience we discover that many of our fears are unfounded.

Absolute priority of acknowledgement of help received is to my wife, Lyn. All round assistance from her is beyond calculation. She, together with her helpers, manage all the affairs of the bi-monthly magazine *Reformation Today* and Carey Publications. Keith Weber spent many hours in the first round of proof reading before type-setting. Then our daughter Sharon proof read the galley proofs. I refused some of her suggestions because the preacher in me cannot bear to be over conformed to the stricter demands of grammar and style.

The generosity of the Church at Cuckfield is warmly acknowledged. This local church has always possessed a wide vision and supported a variety of endeavours in promoting the truth to all nations. Lately this has extended to helping in the production of vital literature materials in other languages. This is something which we regard as a tremendous privilege. It is not possible to mention all the names of the members of church and congregation who constantly assist in our literature industry and outreach.

Then I would like to acknowledge the esteemed friendship of our Christian friends from Holland who so often come to encourage us. Peter and Anje Bates, Prof. Douma, Ds. Scholte and many others have prompted an interest to expound the issues contained herein. The fullness of the basis of our unity with non-Baptists is expounded in the chapter with that title.

Pastor Frederic Buhler of Mulhouse has built up a folio of information on baptistries from early centuries. His kindness in sharing some of this information with us is appreciated. The illustrations are grouped together between parts 1 and 2.

Professor Hugh Flemming of St. John in the Maritime Provinces of Canada, together with pastors Dave Sanford of San Diego and Tom Lyon of Tacoma,

Washington State, have given valuable assistance in theological formulation on the subject in question. Especially esteemed is our unity with the churches led by these ministers of the Gospel, a unity which extends to close cooperation and mutual support. Pastor Ron Edmonds of Long Beach, California, while not involved in this particular project, has played no small rôle in encouraging the planting of Reformed Baptist churches along the West Coast of America, which is just one of many areas in the world where the issues explained in this book are extremely relevant.

The fact that appreciation of our Reformation heritage is increasingly appreciated in so many countries is the cause of much encouragement. The contribution of this book as I have explained is a corporate effort. To the few who have been named, the many not mentioned, and above all to him who is the head and sustainer of the universal Church I express hearty gratitude.

Cover picture

Two thirds of the earth's surface is covered with water, thus the ocean is an appropriate way to depict 'many waters' (John 3:23), especially as many baptisms have taken place in the sea. Immersion presupposes the presence of water. Do arid conditions automatically preclude its possibility, as many opponents have argued? Take for example Charles Hodge.[1] When discussing Philip and the Eunuch he argues that literal baptism (immersion) is improbable because of the difficulty in procuring water in the desert and the difficulty of procuring baptismal dress! We nowhere read in Scripture of any need of special dress, and the issue of water is settled by the text. Philip and the Eunuch went down *into* the water and came up *out of* it again.[2] No sane person will go down *into* water if a cupful is all that is necessary.

Hodge finds the baptisms at Pentecost even harder to take literally. He cannot identify any site in Jerusalem where so many could have been immersed. He argues that absence of a large water supply and the physical impractibility of 70 people baptising 3,000 make immersion unlikely. Both arguments are totally hypothetical. Cities cannot function without large supplies of water. Moreoever, the concern shown by the Romans for clean plentiful water supplies and public sanitation was not to be matched until the present modern age. Aqueducts such as the Pont du Gard near Nimes, large public baths such as those at Bath, and similar marvels of engineering and architecture still stand as testimony to the ingenuity of people at that time in this very matter of water supply. There were at least six reservoirs of considerable size in Jerusalem during the first century A.D.,[3] and the rituals of Judaism included the dipping into water of those who were ceremonially unclean.

Nor is the physical strain of immersing believers such as to make a literal understanding of Acts 8 unreasonable. One of the first physical realities discovered by those who immerse is the buoyancy of water, making even multiple baptism not an onerous task. At a leisurely pace it takes two minutes to baptize four people. Twenty-five people could be immersed in as little as fifteen minutes. It would have been quite possible for the 72 of Luke 10 each to have immersed forty or fifty converts. Undoubtedly it was required at Pentecost for all 3,000 to be baptized in one day to emphasize the act of immense grace that had taken place, and to show that the Church of Christ had been initiated with power.

Hodge's next problem is to imagine how Saul of Tarsus could possibly have been immersed at Damascus. He simply presumes that no pools were available, and that Saul, who, 'arising was baptized' would have had no time to find one! Such a presumption is patently absurd. The text declares that Saul was baptized — dipped — and this should be sufficient even though the precise amount of time or the distance travelled between arising from a prostrate position and actual immersion is not specified! In similar hot climates the distance between the lounge and the swimming pool is minimal. We have no warrant to circumscribe the domestic or public arrangements of societies just because they are separated from us by the distance of time.

---

[1] *The Mode and Subjects of Baptism,* Charles Hodge, p. 17.
[2] The prepositions *eis* and *ek* being used with their usual meaning, other words being available if Luke had not wanted readers to understand *into* and *out of.*
[3] *Manual of Theology,* Vol. 2, J. L. Dagg, p. 63.

Contents

Part 1

The Testimony of Baptism

Why a testimony?

1

T HE Lord's Supper is a testimony or declaration. It declares the Lord's death until he comes. Likewise baptism is a testimony or declaration. It tells forth a message.

Thus when Emmanuel entrusted himself to the arms of John the baptizer he did so as a testimony before heaven and earth. It was a testimony approved by his Father for he expressed his good pleasure audibly. It was a testimony owned by the Holy Spirit as he appeared in a visible form. It was a testimony expressing the entire mission of our Lord — his appearance among men, his going down into the waters of destruction, his emergence again to new life (Matt. 3:16, 17).

After he rose from the dead and before his ascension he gave an express command that all believers should give visible expression of sharing their testimony of union with him. Their union with him is to be shown in following him through the waters of baptism. In this way the pattern is to be perpetuated. Every single believer joined to Christ, is joined to him in his life, death and resurrection. Thus every baptism is a fresh unfolding or exhibition of the life of Christ. He has come. The believer trusts in him. The believer follows him into the waters of death, not to perish there, but to identify with Christ's death-agony there, and then to own his victory, because Christ rose victoriously. Now the believer lives in the power of that victory. By baptism the believer is declaring to the universe that he is complete in Christ.

As the Lord's supper testifies to the centralities of Christ's death (poured out wine and broken bread), and life (cleansing wine and life-giving bread), so baptism testifies to Christ's death (burial), and life (resurrection from the tomb).

15

This testimony is not insignificant. It tells forth the story of God's grace. It is a testimony of the Father's love for the Son whom he has given. Christ made himself one with us. He is the gift and provision of the Father. When we see Christ descending into the waves of Jordan we see the gift of heaven there descending. When he comes up again we see the Father's bounty — a bounty which he, the Father, is well pleased to give. This gift was gratuitous. It did not involve obligation. The baptism of Christ is a demonstration of the Father's love because while we were yet sinners Christ was given over to death for us. This is how God showed his love toward us: he sent his one and only Son into the world that we might live through him.

Believer's baptism is no misnomer. It is the believer alone who can testify to faith. When a person has been converted, had his eyes opened, been turned from darkness to light, from Satan to God, from self-service to Christ's service, he declares his new position by baptism. That is his testimony. It is not something he has made up himself. It is an ordinance which originated in God and is provided from heaven. Everything which comes direct from God is perfect. He knew full well that baptism perfectly portrays what the believer needs to say in his testimony.

As Christ went down voluntarily to be submerged, so I voluntarily descend into the water. I am not being forced by anyone to do this. I am desirous to express that my sins have been washed away. I want to show my faith in Christ's substitutionary death for me. I desire to declare my union with him in his death, burial and resurrection. My wish is to declare that I am now in union with the Trinity. I am in Christ, I am a child of God, I am indwelt by the Spirit. All this is declared in my baptism. I am not being brought to the waters. I am not being carried to the stream. I come of my own accord. I come because I believe. It is my faith. True, my faith is God's gift to me. But now it has been given, it is my faith, and by it I wish to declare to the whole of heaven and earth, to my relatives, friends and neighbours, that I repose my whole trust in Christ. I declare to all the world that union with him which is mine.

Baptism is also a testimony of the church. The baptized one is coming into union not only with the head, but with the body. There is only one body of which they are all members; only one Lord whom they all serve; one Father whose children they all are; one Spirit who lives in them all. This too is being declared (Eph. 4:4-6). The whole assembly participates in the baptism by publicly acknowledging the procedure and welcoming the candidate into the brotherhood. From their company who have been instrumental in his conversion, he descends into the river. To their fellowship he returns from the water.

Baptism is also a testimony to the world. Their gaze is not to be discouraged. Our Lord was baptized in public. The baptisms at Pentecost were not secret.

The ordinance is a declaration that we are saving ourselves from this untoward generation. We are leaving, and by faith have already left behind our allegiance to an ungodly world. Baptism declares a new allegiance and union which is well understood by anti-Christian societies. These will not oppose mild friendship with Christians but will oppose vehemently those who declare that they wish to own total union with Christ and his church. Discipleship is costly. Our Lord warned us that it would be so (Matt. 10:32-39).

In addition to all the above, baptism is a testimony to a new life. The old, dark, godless world is abandoned. A new world of light and truth is entered. The old was cursed. The new is blessed. The old is doomed. Even now the new is blossoming and growing. A land flowing with milk and honey awaits us. It is a domain in which all things are being made new — a new city with new mansions, rich fellowship, exalted worship. There is a new earth to explore and a new universe to enjoy. Baptism declares the newness of life in which God himself will be our God and in which all the riches he gives us will reflect his glory and evoke our praise.

The testimony of the new testament to baptism

2

THE baptism of Jesus forms the basis of the baptism which he commanded for all his disciples. There is the sense in which his baptism is unique. It symbolizes the fulfilment of all righteousness. We could not do that, and in that sense we could not follow him at all. What we do as believers is to acknowledge that the righteousness which he wrought is ours by union with him. That union we express in our baptism which is an exact replica in form of his. He takes the whole load of sin and has it washed away: symbolically in the waters; literally in the baptism of his sufferings and fiery ordeal. Our sins are washed away symbolically by the water and literally by the baptism of Jesus in his sufferings on the Cross as substitute and sin bearer.

The command that all who believe should be baptized in the name of the Trinity is part of the great commission (Matt. 28:18-20). The nations are so to be taught that they come into union with the Trinity by faith, the reality of their spiritual experience proving their faith to be genuine. That union is then to be expressed in the ordinance of baptism. It is for believers, and to this truth all the New Testament gives testimony. The new covenant is coextensive with all who know the Lord from the least to the greatest, 'for I will forgive their wickedness, and will remember their sins no more' (Heb. 8:11, 12). That presupposes the necessity of faith.

Consistent with this is the fact that the book of Acts reports that every person who repented and believed was baptized; the 3,000 at Pentecost (Acts 2:41), the converts at Samaria (Acts 8:12, 13) including Simon the Sorceror (who turned out to be false, which shows that mistakes about conversion in no way invalidate the principle of baptizing on the basis of a credible profession of faith), the Ethiopian Eunuch (Acts 8:36-39), Saul of Tarsus (Acts 9:17, 18), the household of Cornelius (Acts 10:47, 48), the household of Lydia (Acts 16:14, 15), the household of the Philippian gaoler (Acts 16:31-33), the household of Crispus, many Corinthians (Acts 18:8), and the disciples at Ephesus (Acts 19:5).

Note that several households believed. We know this to be the case with Cornelius because they received the Holy Spirit. It may have been a considerable company who had been influenced by the example of Cornelius as he sought to follow God according to the Old Testament, for we read that Peter addressed 'a large gathering of people' (Acts 10:27). In the case of Lydia it is likely that hers was a working household, perhaps a miniature factory, as she was a businesswoman apparently producing and selling purple cloth. The manufacturing aspect is only one of conjecture and we cannot know for certain the exact nature of her household or companions. In the case of Crispus we are told that 'his entire household' believed. Paul baptized individuals such as Crispus and Gaius, and also a household (Stephanas, 1 Cor. 16:15). Nothing is said of the families belonging to the twelve believers at Ephesus. If the idea of baptizing the children including babes, together with the believing head, was an inviolable principle, would not Paul have waited for the families of these men to be gathered?

The one place where children are included is Acts 2:39. The promised gift of the Holy Spirit is to the children of those who will believe. These children, it seems to be implied, are near at hand. The same promise is to all who believingly embrace the Gospel, even though they may be far away. Then comes the crucial qualifying clause, 'all whom the Lord our God will call'; which presupposes the gift of faith.

There are those who seize the idea of households and insist that there must have been infants or young children included. Not one such is mentioned in the text. Concerning the baptism of infants silence reigns. If only one case could be discovered it would prove the case for infant baptism.

The New Testament is not silent, as we have shown in the case of Acts 2:39 above. Nevertheless many take the presumed silence as an absolute presumption that all infants would automatically be included with their parents. After all, women are never mentioned yet are automatically included at the communion table. To this we reply that of course women are included, but only if they are believers; and so may children be included in baptism and at the Table, *but only if they are believers*. The terms of the great commission are perfectly clear. These are the terms of the new covenant which is emphatically different in its administration from the Old (Heb. 8:9ff.). To qualify you must know the Lord and have your sins forgiven.

If this matter is as plain as dayshine to us, and to many generations of Christians, why should we suppose that it would not be equally plain to those who receive the identical instructions from our Lord, especially since they had already experienced and become accustomed to a baptism which was designed for repentant sinners, that is, the baptism of John and the baptism of Jesus (Jn. 4:1, 2).

Furthermore we always stress that 'all' in Scripture is not always to be taken literally. That would be to make the Bible ridiculous. 'All Judea' (Matt. 3:5) going out to hear John does not mean every single one. We must insist on the right of general expression in every language. For instance in Paul's reference to the household of Stephanas it would have been pedantic to say that Lucius was on holiday, Myra was too young and aunt Celia was ill.

The commission of our Lord is confirmed not only by the examples we have throughout the book of Acts, but also by the teaching of the epistles.

There is only one baptism:

> There is one body and one Spirit — just as you were called to one hope when you were called — one Lord, one faith, *one baptism;* one God and Father of all, who is over all and through all and in all (Eph. 4:4-6).

It is a baptism into the Trinity upon faith and repentance which is the only way in which Ephesians 4:4-6 can be interpreted. All those addressed are called. All are responsible for the unity of the Holy Spirit already possessed in the bond of peace. All enjoy union with the Trinity. All exercise the same hope and all are living members of the same body. All these features apply to believers only. Observe the important position given to believers' baptism at the centre of Paul's appeal for unity in the church.

Baptism is the confirmation of regeneration, regeneration being the baptism of the Holy Spirit which brings the believer into union with Christ, this union finding its expression in the faith of the believer. This is the express teaching of Galatians 3:25-28.

> Now that faith has come, we are no longer under the supervision of the law. You are all sons of God through faith in Christ Jesus, for all of you who were baptized into Christ have been clothed with Christ. There is neither Jew nor Greek, slave nor free, male nor female, for you are all one in Christ Jesus.

The baptism into Christ goes with the putting on of Christ. Research has revealed that with Jewish proselyte baptism it was essential that every part of the body was to be in contact with the water. Apparently Christians followed this idea. Apparently there was a stripping off of the old garments, the naked one immersed, and then a white robe was placed on the candidate as he emerged from the water, a symbol of being clothed with Christ.[1] I am not suggesting that we should follow this routine but rather making the observation that the 'being clothed with Christ' was a meaningful reference to baptism for the early Christians.

John's baptism was one which represented washing, which concept is carried over and included in Christian baptism. However, the momentous and primary concept of union dominates in the meaning and testimony of believers' baptism. There are two passages which confirm this, namely, Romans 6:1-6 and Colossians 2:11-13.

Romans 6:1-6 describes in detail the significance and meaning of baptism. It is union with Christ in the entire sequence of his saving work, life, death, burial, resurrection and session at God's right hand. For emphasis we will underline the verbs in the past tense.

> What shall we say, then? Shall we go on sinning, so that grace may increase? By no means! We died to sin; how can we live in it any longer? Or don't you know that all of us who were baptized into Christ Jesus were baptized into his death? We were therefore buried with him through baptism into death in order that, just as Christ was raised from the dead through the glory of the Father, we too may live a new life. If we have been united with him in his death, we will certainly also be united with him in his resurrection. For we know that our old self was crucified with him so that the body of sin might be rendered powerless, that we should no longer be slaves to sin.

The most striking feature in this passage is not that the believer in his baptism is laid in his own grave, but that through that action he is set alongside Christ in his.[2] This is something that has happened in the past. So close is the identification that it is as though everything that happened to Christ happened to the believer. These historic and momentous happenings were enacted in our immersion. The consistent use of the aorist (past tense) emphasises this:

> we died to sin (verse 2)

> all of us who were baptized into Christ Jesus were baptized into his death (verse 3)

> therefore we were buried with him through baptism into death (verse 4)

> in order that, just as Christ was raised from the dead through the glory of the Father, we too may live a new life (verse 4)

> we have been (perfect tense) united with him in his death we will certainly also be united with him in his resurrection (verse 5)

> our old self was crucified with him (verse 6)

> we died with Christ, we believe we shall also live with him (verse 8)

According to this passage we see in baptism, 1. What happened to Christ, 2. What has happened to the believer for he too has died, has been buried and has been raised again, 3. That this believer is now to live as a new person. He can never be what he was before, because that person has been put to death. All the exhortations that follow in Romans chapter six indicate the reality of the struggle that will ensue, for sinful remnants remain in this new person. Nevertheless, because he has been regenerated and because he is now one with Christ, he can never be what he was before. His baptism proclaims that.

When did the change take place? It took place when by faith he received Christ. Behind his faith, which justifies him and motivates him, is the work of the Holy Spirit in regeneration (Jn. 1:12, 13). His baptism in water is a public demonstration of what has already happened.[3] There is no suggestion in the New Testament that any others except converts had any claim to baptism. The necessity of faith prior to baptism is clearly seen in the second major passage, namely, Colossians 2:11-13.

> In him you were also circumcised, in the putting off of the sinful nature, not with a circumcision done by the hands of men but with the circumcision done by Christ, having been buried with him in baptism and raised with him through your faith in the power of God, who raised him from the dead. When you were dead in your sins and in the uncircumcision of your sinful nature, God made you alive with Christ. He forgave us all our sins.

Note the necessity of faith in the words, *through your faith*. It is by faith that union with Christ has taken place, a union expressed in the burial of baptism. 'Without the exercise of faith, then, there would be no validity in the baptismal act.'[4]

In this passage circumcision is the figure used to remind the believers that their old nature had been cast away. Circumcision was the stripping away and casting away of the foreskin with repugnance, symbolizing the casting away of the old sinful nature. It is through Christ's sufferings that the old carnal person has been done away and by Christ's resurrection that the new man emerges.

We must remember that when Paul reminds believers of their baptism, whether at Rome or Colosse, he is reminding them of something which they actually experienced as believers. When they were plunged into water it was the token of their union with Christ. Paul did not regard baptism as an optional extra. His references in 1 Corinthians 1:14-17 do not mean that baptism was not important, but rather that the baptizer was insignificant. He takes it for granted that all the believers in Corinth were baptized (1 Cor. 1:13; 6:11; 10:1 ff.).[5]

The symbolism of washing in John's baptism is carried over into Christian baptism. The baptism administered by the disciples of Jesus (Jn. 4:1 ff.) probably signified the washing away of sin and the forgiveness that would accompany that. It is unlikely that our Lord would have initiated the full symbolism of Christian baptism before the completion of his work on the Cross which would invest it with its foremost meaning. He was content to lay the foundations of baptism, the full meaning of which would emerge later.

The idea of washing is sustained in Acts 22:16, 1 Peter 3:21, Hebrews 10:22 and 1 Corinthians 6:11. The same word wash *(apolouō)* is used in Acts 22:16 and 1 Corinthians 6:11.

The subject of the giving of the Holy Spirit and sealing is related to believers' baptism; but I will not press that matter here, as enough evidence has been presented to prove that baptism is prominent in the New Testament. It is the momentous character of this ordinance commanded by the head of the church that Paul uses to humble the Corinthian schismatics. To be baptized into the name of Christ (his name stands for all his attributes) is a supreme privilege. 'What!' declares Paul, 'were you baptized into my name? Was I crucified for you?' How detestable the idea! He is shaming them by reminding them of the greatness of their union with Christ, which union was expressed in their baptism, and which should automatically forbid divisions because there was only one Lord to cleave to.

In concluding this perspective of the testimony given to baptism by the New Testament, it may be helpful to answer a question which often perplexes Christians. Why is it that believers in the book of Acts are reported as being baptized in the name of Jesus and not expressly in the name of the Trinity? (Acts 10:48; 19:5). As has been shown, the Lord Jesus is absolutely central in baptism. It is because of his victory that the gift of the Holy Spirit has been given to all believers, and by him that we are brought into union with the Father. We need not be pedantic about it. Luke was not required to state everything in every narrative. To be baptized into the name of Jesus is put for the whole. Not for one moment would we think that the Trinitarian formula would have been forgotten in the actual rite of baptism. To be baptized into Christ was to be baptized into the Trinity.

[1] *Baptism in the New Testament,* Beasley-Murray, p. 148.
[2] *ibid.,* p. 130.
[3] *New Testament Theology,* Donald Guthrie, p. 755.
[4] *ibid.,* p. 756.
[5] *Romans,* F. F. Bruce, p. 136.

The testimony of
immersion to baptism

3

ALEXANDER CARSON (1776-1844) was an outstanding minister who was ordained into the ministry at the exceptional age of 18. He ministered for 50 years in a small village of only 2,000 people called Tubbermore in Northern Ireland. During that time he was challenged by members of the church to examine whether it was scriptural to sprinkle infants for baptism. His subsequent studies led him to renounce the practice. Although a man of meek and charitable disposition this renunciation of human tradition brought upon him the wrath of his denomination. A delegation was sent to thrust him from the pulpit. He requested their restraint until he had completed his sermon. As he was leaving one of the congregation raised his Bible aloft and proclaimed, 'Let all who wish to follow the Bible come this way.' The meeting house was immediately emptied.

That day in a green field nearby 16 covenanted to form a new church. For some time they worshipped in the open air, then in a barn, and ultimately built a new sanctuary. Over the decades which followed spiritual blessings accumulated until the total baptized membership reached 500. All these were local residents.

These details are not recounted to score a point, because all controversy has dreadful potential for damage, and should only be entered into if the conscience will not allow otherwise, and only if conducted in love and the fear of Jehovah. The account is included here as an outstanding example of a minister who was prospered in the devotion of his entire ministry to one restricted locality.

Alexander Carson is reputed to be the genius behind the outstanding commentary by his intimate friend Robert Haldane. The Haldane manuscripts were apparently edited and expanded by him. Carson wrote a fine book on

Esther, but his most famous production was *Baptism, its Mode and its Subjects.* This was a work of 237 pages.

The author began this work with a detailed study of the meaning of the word 'to baptize'. His method was first to establish the mode of baptism. He devoted 169 pages to this and the remaining 68 pages to the subjects of baptism. This means that over 70% of Carson's work was devoted to the mode, and less than 30% to the subjects of baptism.

Now was this man who displayed exceptional ability and sound judgment mistaken in this disproportion? The technical nature of the first section would certainly seem to militate against its popularity yet the volume has played a major role in establishing the scriptural validity of believer's baptism. I have tried to understand why Carson set out to prove immersion to be synonymous with baptism. In analysing this we have to remember that Carson was nurtured in the Westminster Confession of Faith. The 28th chapter of the Confession reads as follows:

1. Baptism is a sacrament of the New Testament, ordained by Jesus Christ, not only for the solemn admission of the party baptized into the visible church; but also, to be unto him a sign and seal of the covenant of grace, of his ingrafting into Christ, of regeneration, of remission of sins, and of his giving up of himself unto God, through Jesus Christ, to walk in newness of life. Which sacrament is, by Christ's own appointment, to be continued in his Church until the end of the world.

2. The outward element to be used in this sacrament is water, wherewith the party is to be baptized, in the name of the Father, and of the Son, and of the Holy Ghost, by a minister of the Gospel, lawfully called thereunto.

The above paragraphs are clear statements with which we would agree wholeheartedly. Ingrafting into Christ and union with the Trinity are declared faithfully. However, the clauses which follow read like this:

3. Dipping of the person into the water is not necessary; but baptism is rightly administered by pouring, or sprinkling water upon the person.

4. Not only those that do actually profess faith in and obedience unto Christ, but also the infants of one, or both, believing parents, are to be baptized.

Paragraph 3 deprives the ordinance of its proper Biblical expression and paragraph 4 opens the door to a premature application of the ordinance whereby it is nullified for all those to whom it is so applied.

The central meaning conveyed in the symbolic expressiveness of baptism into Christ (burial and rising again) is removed by the substitution of pouring or sprinkling which can never symbolize union. It is the same as saying that we can substitute bread and wine in the communion with breathing. That is to say, two gulps of air for the bread and three for the wine will do. I am not saying that the ordinances of Christ are utterly dependent upon certain elements. In the case of a primitive tribe in New Guinea the missionaries used goat's milk for wine and yams for bread, until such time as the people came to know what bread and wine were.

Immersion was employed as the mode of baptism at the beginning but pouring gradually became more popular. This in turn was reduced to sprinkling, and now to be sure a little moistening would not be objected to. If a minute amount of water is adequate, why not pass the thumb over the tongue and apply it to the brow of the infant?

What was intended in the first place as a fully adequate expression to illustrate a momentous and illustrious union has been rendered meaningless. The mode has been reduced to an absolute minimum. The Gospel narratives tell of Jesus coming up out of the river Jordan. What began with a river can now be contained in a little bottle! One would think that the world's reservoirs had dried up, or that the oceans vastnesses were no more!

Immersion has a unique testimony to give to the ordinance of believer's baptism. It and it alone conveys and denotes the message intended, namely, union with Christ together with the washing away of sin. We can now appreciate the concern of Alexander Carson to defend immersion as the correct mode of baptism.

Then we observe that the ordinance is destroyed by the assertion that not believers only but also 'infants of one, or both, believing parents, are to be baptized'. By including infants the sacrament or ordinance is brought to nothing for the simple reason, that should these infants, when they are come to years repent and believe, there is no ordinance for them whereby their newly found union with Christ by faith can be expressed. For them it does not exist. If one should come forward and ask to be baptized as a believer, he is given to understand that although it never registered in his conscious experience, that baptism has transpired already. The applicant believer, the church that has nurtured him, the angels who rejoice over every repentant sinner, all are deprived of the ordinance.

Believer's baptism was designed to celebrate the meaningful content of the above cited Westminster Confession, chapter 28, clause 1. But in the case of the infant we have no profession whatever to test, no testimony to hear, no witness to observe, no understanding or experimental knowledge to examine: nothing! The good wishes, ardent prayers and fervent hopes of believing parents are no substitute for the articles of faith and repentance. Experience and discernment of religious experience are the coinage and business of New Testament Christianity. We hardly need to quote scripture texts to prove this. Whole books such as Romans, 1 Peter, Hebrews and the first epistle of John have to do with faith, justification, assurance and perseverance (see Chapter 12). Believer's baptism is the consummation of the new covenant. The proof of the new covenant is that a person shows that the writing of God's laws have been engraved on his mind and heart. He now knows, experiences, evidences and witnesses to the momentous fact that God is his God through Christ by the Spirit. Immersion alone is the visible representation of entrance or initiation into the Trinity and into the Christian Church.

What does the word 'baptize' mean?
Thayer's Greek Lexicon says the word means 'to dip repeatedly, to immerse, submerge (of vessels sunk)'. An explanation follows, 'In the N.T. it is used particularly of the rite of sacred ablution, first instituted by John the Baptist, afterwards by Christ's command received by Christians and adjusted to the contents and nature of their religion (see baptisma), viz. an immersion in water, performed as a sign of the removal of sin, and administered to those who, impelled by a desire for salvation, sought admission to the benefits of the Messiah's kingdom.'

According to the Dictionary of N.T. Theology *baptō* means to dip, and *baptizō* means to dip, immerse, submerge, baptize and *baptismos:* dipping, washing (Vol. 1, p. 144 ff.).

The word *baptizō* is never used to signify pouring or sprinkling for the simple reason that those actions have their own specific words, namely, *ekcheō* — I pour, and *rhantizō* — I sprinkle. To the Greek speaking people today *baptizō*, to baptize, has only one meaning and that is to immerse. This is why the Greek Orthodox Church practises immersion for their infants. To them baptism literally means to dip or submerge. Their own language preserves the correctness of the word even if tradition has supplanted the Biblical requirement that only believers qualify for immersion.

When we examine the New Testament we find that *baptizō* is always used in the same consistent way as the Greeks use it, namely to dip, immerse or submerge. T. J. Conant produced a treatise in 1865. His purpose was to prove and illustrate that for eight centuries surrounding our Lord's ministry, the Greek word *baptizō* meant to dip or immerse exclusively. Conant from Greek literature cites 236 cases in context to prove his case.

Immediately there comes to mind, however, such references as 1 Corinthians 10:2, 'They were all baptized into Moses in the cloud and in the sea.' Surely the one thing that did not happen was the immersion of the Israelites into the Red Sea! The difficulty is quickly resolved if we attempt to use the substitutes. We cannot say they were all sprinkled into Moses or the cloud or the sea. Nor could they have been poured in. They were immersed into Moses.

This means they were identified with him in every possible way and submerged into that salvation experience in the sea and the cloud. The word is used as a powerful metaphor to denote totality. There can be no substitute. This is expounded in more detail in the excursus.

Likewise, our Lord was submerged in sufferings. He did not say to his disciples, 'can you be poured with the sufferings that I am poured with?' or, 'are you able to be sprinkled with the sufferings that I am sprinkled with?' Rather, 'can you be submerged in the sufferings I am submerged in?' Again a most powerful meaning denoting totality is conveyed by the word baptism. It is used as a metaphor, and here again no substitute is adequate. Once more the reader's attention is invited to the excursus on 'baptism' as a metaphor.

The word immersion can be substituted for baptism wherever it is found in the New Testament without any distortion or artificiality resulting. The reason for this is that in the Greek it means precisely to immerse, dip or submerge. That is a concept which denotes something total and complete. 'John,' said Jesus, 'I indeed immerse you in water for repentance, but after me will come one who will immerse you in the Holy Spirit.' The Holy Spirit was poured out in the day of Pentecost and the place was filled where they were sitting.

Are there exceptions to this meaning of submerge? If there are we can be sure there will be those who will seize the exception to make it the rule. This partly explains why Alexander Carson was fastidious in his study of the history and usage of the words of which there are two: 1. *Baptō* which means to dip or dye. It also means to dip into a dye, and also draw water. 2. *Baptizō* was an intensive form of *baptō* which means to dip, submerge or immerse, but is also used to convey the idea of perishing in the sense of a man who is drowned and a ship which is sunk. Thus Siculus speaking of animals says, 'Many of the land animals immersed (baptized) in the river perish.'

Let us now turn to the very important matter of New Testament usage. *Baptō* occurs four times only (twice in John 13:26, and then in Luke 16:24 and Revelation 19:13). In every case the meaning simply is to dip.

The verb *baptizō* is used in 21 passages in Acts, always in reference to Christian baptism of believers with three exceptions which refer to John's baptism. The verb also occurs in Romans 6:3, nine times in 1 Corinthians and once in Galatians 3:27. The noun is used in the Gospels to describe John's baptism, and in Romans 6:4, Ephesians 4:5, Colossians 2:12 and 1 Peter 3:21 to describe Christian baptism.

In the LXX *baptō* is used about ten times to denote dip. *Baptizō* is used four times, once in Isaiah 21:4 to denote destruction, the others to describe Naaman's sevenfold submersion in the river Jordan.

The noun *baptisma* is peculiar to the New Testament alone and must therefore be interpreted in the light of the New Testament alone. It is erroneous to proceed to a point outside the New Testament for our starting point.

From a study of all the references only one conclusion can be made and that is that baptism has its own unique meaning. We ought not to tamper with it or attempt to use substitutes. To be baptized into Christ and into his body conveys the idea of complete union. Washing and sprinkling which terms have their own testimony will be studied separately. In the meantime let us acknowledge the unique testimony of immersion.

The distinct testimony of sprinkling not to be confused with immersion

4

CHARLES HODGE and Nigel Lee are among many anti-Baptist writers who confuse sprinkling with baptism. With distinct and separate Greek words readily available the Holy Spirit, who is the infallible author of Scripture, would have used *rhantizō* (sprinkling), if that was his intention.

Sprinkling has its own separate, distinct and powerful testimony. To discover its roots and meaning we have to go back to the Levitical provisions. There was the sprinkling of blood and there was the sprinkling of water. Since the former has the prominence we will consider it first.

To shed blood is to take life (Rom. 3:15). Blood is essential to human life. Hence to shed blood in Scripture is used as an expression to denote the taking of life (Rom. 3:15, Heb. 12:4). Because life depends on the circulation of blood the word blood in Scripture conveys the fact that life is in the blood. Without the shedding of blood — the forfeiting of life for life — there can be no remission of sin (Heb. 9:22).

In many places the New Testament stresses the necessity of the shedding of the blood of Christ. This truth is central (Rom. 3:25, 1 Cor. 10:16, 11:27, Eph. 2:13, Heb. 9:11-14, 10:19, 1 Pet. 1:2, 1 Jn. 1:7, Rev. 7:14, 12:11).

All the sacrifices point to the one great and final offering which our Lord made of himself (Heb. 10:12-14). The manner in which the blood of the Levitical sacrifices was employed illustrates the efficacy of Christ's atonement. The blood was sprinkled on the mercy seat (literally *propitiatory*, Heb. 9:5) indicating satisfaction made to the demands of the law. The propitiatory was the top of the ark made of acacia wood and covered with gold. On each side formed in gold and attached to the covering was an angel or cherubim, gazing down upon the place where satisfaction was recorded by the sprinkling of blood. The ark contained the tables of the law which summarize all moral requirements. Every sin is a transgression of this moral law in one way or another. Every sin cries for vengeance and the death of the transgressor. But Christ has died. He has made atonement with his blood. He has entered into the holiest of all where the ark is kept and made satisfaction once and for all with his own blood (Heb. 9:11-14).

The blood was sprinkled not only on the propitiatory by the high priest but on the people themselves (Ex. 24:8). Sprinkling was the mode used. In some instances blood was poured at the base of the altar (Ex. 29:12; Lev. 4:7). In the case of the Passover a bunch of hyssop was to be taken and dipped into the blood which had been collected in a basin and then applied to the top and both sides of the door frame. 'When the LORD goes through the land to strike down the Egyptians, he will see the blood on the top and sides of the door-frame and he will pass over that doorway, and he will not permit the destroyer to enter your houses and strike you down' (Ex. 12:23).

The object of the exercise of splashing or applying the blood was visual. It was demonstrative of a momentous fact. *Atonement had been made.* The blood spoke of that. Whether sprinkled on a person, on the mercy seat, splashed with hyssop on lintels and side posts of doors, or poured against the altar, or applied to the horns of the altar of incense (Ex. 30:10), or to the horns of the four corners of the altar of sacrifice (Lev. 16:18), it was in every case an operation of display or demonstration. The idea was one of visual application. The fact of atonement made by blood was now seen. It asserts that the LORD will see the blood (Ex. 12:23). The people will see its testimony. The LORD will see its testimony and be merciful (Ex. 12:23).

Before going on to investigate the meaning of the water of purification let us consider the difference between sprinkling, splashing, smearing or pouring blood on the one hand, and immersion in water on the other. The latter is demonstrating union and washing: the former is proving atonement. It is true that the atonement removes guilt. It cleanses in the forensic sense of satisfying the demands of the law. That is its first meaning. The efficacy lies in the life that has been taken from the victim. It is important to distinguish matters which differ, otherwise the whole exercise of provision of different modes is made meaningless.

Plunging in water was a Hebrew concept, as was washing with water (Lev. 14:8). Aaron and his sons washed their hands and feet with water from the bronze basin (Ex. 30:17 ff.). In contrast, blood was sprinkled.

The concept of sprinkling of the blood is carried over to the New Testament in which we are left in no doubt that Christ's blood alone is efficacious for cleansing of guilt. We are sprinkled by his blood (1 Pet. 1:2; Heb. 12:24). The word selected by the Holy Spirit is *sprinkled.* We are not baptized by or into his blood.

The cleansing power of the blood is pictured vividly in Revelation 7:14, 'These are they who have come out of the great tribulation; they have washed their robes and made them white in the blood of the Lamb.'

We turn now to consider the waters of purification. Numbers chapter 19 describes the red heifer which was to be sacrificed as a whole burnt offering. Again this is mightily expressive of our all-sufficient saviour who was our burnt offering. Needless to say, the heifer was to be without defect or blemish and was never to have been under a yoke — in other words, reserved only for the supreme purpose of sacrifice.

After the burning the ashes were to be gathered up to be mixed with water which was called the water of cleansing for the purification of sin. This water was used in ceremonial cleansing not only for people, but for objects which had become defiled such as tents and furnishings. Hyssop was used to sprinkle or shake the water upon the objects.

In this connection the reference we find in Ezekiel 36:25 is relevant. There Ezekiel sees the water of purification in an eschatological sense pointing to the momentous all-effectual cleansing which was to come in the last times. Here Ezekiel enters the new creation, for directly following (or perhaps simultaneous with) the application of this water by sprinkling comes the new heart and new spirit which is regeneration. The old heart of sin is removed. A new disposition to love God and his laws is given, but never without the prior application of the whole atonement of Christ represented in the ashes of the red heifer. First the Holy Spirit applies Christ's atonement to the believer and then he creates him anew. As suggested above, these may be simultaneous; but certainly we could never entertain the thought that the Holy Spirit will recreate sinners and unite them to Christ without first applying to them the merits of Christ's death. All those for whom Christ died will be sprinkled with the water of purification, and all so sprinkled will be born again.

Thus in John 3:5 Jesus declares, 'I tell you the truth, unless a man is born of water and the Spirit, he cannot enter the kingdom of God.' To a Hebrew like Nicodemus, an accomplished teacher possessing a profound knowledge of the Mosaic rites, this could only mean the water of purification.

George Smeaton in his book on the Holy Spirit (p. 169 ff.) declares that 'this water to which our Lord refers CERTAINLY REGENERATES'. The capital letters are his not ours, but we agree with the emphasis. Baptismal waters never regenerate, but included in the symbolism of believer's baptism is the immersion of that person into Christ and into the body of Christ by the Spirit, which runs parallel with regeneration. This Paul describes as creation in Christ in Ephesians 2:10.

In application of this we must note that the flowing waters of baptism are flowing waters of washing or ablution. These have nothing whatever to do with the ceremonial water mixed with the ashes of the red heifer. The ceremonial waters were a mixture of ashes and water, thus exhibiting their own distinct testimony, the testimony of a life slain and wholly offered up in the fires of God's wrath. There is not the remotest connection between the sprinkling with hyssop of this water of atonement and the waters of Jordan in which Naaman dipped seven times, and in which John baptized our Lord.

Desperate then is the reasoning by anti-Baptist writers like Charles Hodge and Nigel Lee when they confuse the distinct and powerful testimony of sprinkling with that of the equally demonstrative testimony of union by immersion and washing by plunging the body in water.

The distinct testimony
of washing in baptism

So far we have seen that sprinkling possessed its own particular meaning and gave out its own distinct message of atonement accomplished. Immersion tells forth the fact of union accomplished in Christ's death, burial and resurrection. In other words, it has a precise testimony of its own.

We turn now to washing in water. The cleansing power in the sprinkling of the water mixed with the ashes of the red heifer lay in the ashes representing the atoning power of the entire burnt offering. In the case of the running water it is the ablutionary effect of running water that portrays or symbolizes the removal of sin. In Jewish proselyte baptisms the water to be used was to be 'living' if possible. Nakedness was demanded in order that there be no impediment to the washing effect of the water.[1] Washing for ritual purification was common among ancient peoples of the Orient. The Qumran sect was accustomed to washings which apparently involved immersion.[2] Aaron had to bathe his body in water before putting on his holy garments (Lev. 16:4). Purification by washing in water was required after sexual intercourse (Lev. 15), menstruation and birth (Lev. 15), after contact with leprosy (Lev. 13, 14) and with death (Num. 5:1 ff.; 19:11 ff.).

Hebrews 10:22 refers to the sprinkling of our hearts and our bodies having been washed with pure water. The verbs 'having been sprinkled', and 'having been bathed', are perfect participles pointing to the existence of a present state through a past effective action.

Unquestionably the Hebrew readers of the Hebrew epistle would understand by their own cultic language both the purification to which the Levitical priests were subject at the entrance of the Tent of Meeting where they were washed with water (Ex. 29:4), and the sprinkling of the blood upon them which followed (Ex. 29:21). The equivalent of all this in the new convenant administration is that our hearts have been sprinkled by the blood of Christ and made anew (regenerated) by that action once and for all. Following this our bodies have been washed in pure (*Kath" = clean) water. This baptism of washing is something that has been done once and for all but which nevertheless continues to bear a testimony. Hence the perfect participle *having been washed.*

Lest there be any misunderstanding, Peter clarifies this in his letter (1 Pet. 3:21), 'and this water symbolizes baptism that now saves you also — not the removal of dirt from the body but the pledge of a good conscience towards God. It saves you by the resurrection of Jesus Christ.'

Noah and his family came through the waters of destruction by virtue of their place in the ark. By that means they were brought to a new world of resurrection. Christ in his sufferings passed through a deluge to be raised from the dead. We, being joined to Christ (who is an ark most suitable for all God's Noahs), arrive with him in the resurrection world. Now we look back at our baptism and view those waters as waters of destruction through which we have come in Christ. By those waters of destruction all our sins have been washed away — not external dirt — but spiritually we have been washed once and for all.

Thus Paul was commanded to be baptized to represent his union with Christ and the removal thereby of his guilt. Said Ananias, 'And now what are you waiting for? Get up, be baptized and wash your sins away, calling on his name' (Acts 22:16).

The absolute sovereignty of God in regeneration is declared in a number of Scriptures such as John 1:12, 13; Ephesians 2:10; 1 Peter 1:3; and John 3:8. Titus 3:5 also bears testimony to regeneration which essentially precedes that which confirms it, namely, baptism. 'He saved us through the washing of rebirth and renewal by the Holy Spirit.'

There is in the omnipotent act of regeneration a washing away of the guilt and enmity of sin. We are made anew. The old heart is removed. A new heart is created, a heart to know and love God. We can never again be what we were before. Old fleshly inclinations may remain but that does not alter the fact that we are new creatures in Christ.

The context in each case of the texts cited shows that these references and descriptions can only apply to those who can pray (Acts 22:16), who have knowingly had their consciences cleansed (Heb. 10:22), whose hearts have been changed (Ez. 36:26), who have been born again (Jn. 3:8), who know that they have come through the waters of destruction with Christ and have the pledge of a good conscience toward God (1 Pet. 3:21), who know that they have been saved through regeneration by God's mercy, have received the Holy Spirit, have been justified by his grace and have become heirs of the hope of eternal life (Tit. 3:5).

All these texts are addressed to believers. Especially is this true of Titus 3:5. Yet in the Commentary by Jamieson, Fausset and Brown we read, 'infants are *charitably presumed* (italics theirs) to have received a grace in connection with their Christian descent. They are *presumed* (again their italics) to be then regenerated.'[3] In response to this, we would say that such an idea is indeed presumption from first to last. Regeneration can never be presumed for anyone. Peter applies the teaching to those for whom regeneration has become a reality. For them and them alone the visible symbol of washing the body is meaningful.

Yet a further testimony of washing in baptism is that of 1 Corinthians 6:11, 'But you were washed, you were sanctified, you were justified in the name of the Lord Jesus Christ and by the Spirit of our God.' The aorist tense, middle voice *(apelousasthe)*, 'you had yourself washed from your sins,' indicates a voluntary submission on the part of the believer. 'In the name of the Lord Jesus and by the Spirit of our God' reminds us of the baptismal formula, union with Christ and the work of the Spirit. The use of the term *washing* in this context concurs with the use of the term in the other contexts that have been discussed. It is interesting to observe that the majority of exegetes agree with the view that this is a reference to baptism. That being so, let us remember to whom it applies, not infants but former adulterers, homosexuals, thieves, gluttons and blasphemers (1 Cor. 6:10).

[1] *Baptism in the N.T.,* G. R. Beasley-Murray, p. 28.
[2] *Dictionary of N.T. Theology,* Vol. 1, p. 15 ff.
[3] p. 1389.

The testimony of John's baptism

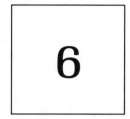

6

JOHN is described as the *baptistes* (the immerser) in the Gospels of Matthew, Luke and Mark. We must not underestimate the place and importance of this greatest of the prophets until that time (Matt. 11:9-15). He came to prepare the way. He was the fulfilment of Isaiah 40:3, 4 — 'A voice of one calling: "In the desert prepare the way for the LORD." '

The ministry of John is embodied in the immersion he administered. This ministry was two-fold. First, it called the people to repentance and faith. 'He went into all the country around the Jordan, preaching a baptism of repentance for the forgiveness of sins' (Luke 3:3). He also proclaimed the necessity of believing in the Son (Jn. 3:22-36). In the baptism administered to those who came forward in repentance lay the assurance of the washing away of sin and consequent forgiveness. His was a baptism of repentance for the forgiveness of sins (Mk. 1:4). Secondly, his baptism in water anticipated a baptism in the Holy Spirit, a baptism which would come from the Messiah accompanied by fire. Thus a place in the Kingdom of Jesus was assured to those who submitted to John's baptism. All those so baptized could anticipate the gift of the Holy Spirit which promise was fulfilled when Christ sent the Spirit by fire and effusion at Pentecost. The fire suggests a fire that the Messiah would employ for the purification and refinement of his people (Is. 4:2-5; Mal. 3:1-6).

John's stress upon genuine repentance is seen in the reformation of life upon which he insisted — sharing of clothes and food, justice in tax-collection, fair dealing on the part of the soldiers.

The area in which John the immerser laboured has given rise to speculation as to his knowledge of and acquaintance with groups or sects like the Essenes. One of these groups was the Qumran community responsible for the Dead Sea scrolls. It has been suggested that it is impossible that John could have been ignorant of their existence. The Qumran community practised baptisms in the Jordan and thought of themselves as preparers of the way of the Lord. They repeated their baptisms and regarded them as washings for the cleansing away of sin but were aware of the fact that going down into the water could not of itself cleanse without repentance.[1] Note the remarkable likeness between John and this sect situated in the same geographic area. But there were also marked differences between John and the Qumran community. John baptized individuals once only. John was appointed to fulfil a unique rôle as a prophet with a specific task as preparer and forerunner. For this he was given great powers of spiritual unction and discernment. Thus John spoke with an authority and finality which the Essenes did not possess.

We cannot tell how the Qumran community came to practise their lustrations or baptisms. That they learned the custom from Jewish proselyte baptism has been conjectured but not proved. It appears that the scholars have searched in vain to find references to Jewish proselyte baptisms earlier than AD 67.[2] The school of Shammai maintained that the proselyte should immerse himself and consume his Passover offering on the same evening. This information comes from a date of about AD 90. Uncertainty surrounds the whole debate of the origins of Jewish proselyte custom. What can be proved is that Jewish practice was undergoing modification while the Christian Church was being established but that gives us no help about the actual origins of the practice.

The Jews prescribed the amount of water to be used (that is that it be adequate), that it should be 'living', by which we would presume it to be fresh running water rather than stagnant, that it should be cold rather than warm and that nothing should impede the waters upon the body of the immersed. In other words, it was required that the candidate be naked.

How much of this pertained in John's baptism we are not able to determine. We can prove that there was plenty of water (Jn. 3:23), that in the case of the river Jordan it was fresh and running.

The main lesson to be derived from all these considerations has to do with lustration or ceremonial cleansing by washing. That is the central idea. Hence the amount of water used, its freshness and the contact of the whole body with the water was important.

The washing away of sins is the concept central to the whole idea of Jewish Proselyte baptism. We can be sure that this idea was likewise central in John's baptism. It is carried over into Christian baptism as we see in Paul's testimony when he recalls the ministry of Ananias who said to him, 'And now what are you waiting for? Get up, be baptized and wash your sins away, calling on his name' (Acts 22:16). This removal of the guilt of sin is dependant on the main factor of Christ's atoning death. This Christian baptism now fully signifies.

When we read the Levitical laws about sexual impurities, menstruation or defilement caused by touching dead bodies we can more readily appreciate that the Jews thought much in terms of bodily impurities being removed by their ceremonial ablutions. Hence Peter declares that water of baptism is symbolic and is not the removal of dirt from the body but rather the pledge of a good conscience toward God.

In retrospect we can summarize by saying that John's form of baptism of plunging sinners into running waters was not new. It was a concept familiar to the Jews and practised frequently by sects in the area of the Jordan and the Dead Sea. John used this mode, and by the authority given him as the forerunner of our Lord invested it with unique importance as a symbol of forgiveness of sin and the cleansing away of guilt in anticipation of the Messiah who would come and baptize with fire and assure his followers a place in his kingdom.

Our Lord vindicated this baptism by being subject to it himself. The Father and the Holy Spirit in turn vindicated it. Thus our Lord identified himself with repentant sinners who submitted themselves to the terms of John's baptism. In being baptized himself he adopted the mode involved as a symbol of what he himself would accomplish for our salvation in his death and resurrection. By investing baptism with this meaning he now requires that all his disciples identify with him in the same way, that is, by being baptized. Thus John's baptism paved the way for Christian baptism.

[1] *Baptism in the N.T.*, Beasley-Murray, p. 11.
[2] *ibid.*, p. 18.

The testimony of Jesus
in his baptism

MARK, Matthew and Luke report the baptism of Jesus. Each narrator provides distinctive features not told by the others. Mark informs us that as 'Jesus was coming up out of the water, he saw heaven being torn open' (Mk. 1:9, 10). Matthew reports the fact that John tried to deter him, saying, 'I need to be baptized by you, and do you come to me?' Jesus replied, 'Let it be so now; it is proper for us to do this to fulfil all righteousness.' Then John consented (Matt. 3:13-17). Luke tells us that, 'when all the people were being baptized, Jesus was baptized too. And as he was praying, heaven was opened' (Luke 3:21-22).

The apostle John does not describe the actual baptism but reports the testimony of the Baptist who said that he actually saw the Spirit come down from heaven as a dove and remain on Jesus. By that the Baptist knew that Jesus was the one who would baptize with the Holy Spirit (Jn. 3:32-34).

We have already established that John's baptism represented a cleansing away of sin for repentant sinners who could then with confidence rest on the promise of the Holy Spirit who would be given by the now imminent Messiah.

John the Baptist's objection to the baptism of Jesus confirms this. Matthew reports that John tried to deter Jesus on the grounds that the washing was for sinners. John counted himself among sinners but quite rightly discerned that Jesus was different and quite apart. He was the sinless one. We conclude that Jesus' insistence confirms that the baptism was to be interpreted as his identification with sinners. It is significant that he was not baptized in a separate or special service, but, as Luke tells us, 'when all the people were being baptized, Jesus was baptized too'.

Then we have the explanation provided by our Lord reported by Matthew, 'Let it be so now; it is proper for us to do this to fulfil all righteousness.' To fulfil all righteousness denotes that there is no righteousness that will not be met, satisfied or fulfilled by this act of baptism. It represents the entire undertaking of Christ to bear away our sins by submitting to the punishments meted out by God's wrath upon him as sinbearer.

Jeremiah promised that a righteous Branch would be raised up to David whose name would be called The LORD Our Righteousness (Jer. 23:5, 6). This righteousness was fulfilled by our Lord in his submission to the law. 'I have not come to abolish the Law or the Prophets: I have not come to abolish them but to fulfil them' (Matt. 5:17). He was born under the Law (Gal. 4:4). The Law or ten commandments, two of which are immediately expounded in the above-mentioned context of Matthew 5:17, have terrific power to search out, detect and condemn any transgression whatsoever. It is wonderful to reflect on the fact that Christ was holy, blameless and undefiled and that he did not commit the least sin. It is even more wonderful to think that he not only fulfilled the requirements of the law negatively in not sinning but positively in doing all that was required of him. He loved God perfectly and he loved his neighbours perfectly. Thus he was fully equipped to take up the rôle of sinbearer and be accepted as such. Only a perfect person, only a Lamb without blemish, could be acceptable for the rôle required.

The imputation of this righteousness to sinners who believe in Jesus is the theme and thrust of Paul's letter to the Romans. As we look back to the river Jordan we see a sinless person joining others to be baptized as a sinner alongside sinners. Why? There is only one satisfactory answer and that is that by this action he is becoming a sinner by imputation. By this act of identification with sinners God 'made him who had no sin to be sin for us, so that we might become the righteousness of God' (2 Cor. 5:21).

This act of God the Father reminds us of the voluntary submission of Christ to the Father's will. It reminds us of the eloquent Servant passages of Isaiah which describe the person, ministry, sufferings and subsequent glories of the Servant of Jehovah (42:1-9; 49:1-7; 50:4-11; 52:13 to 53:12).

It is submission that we see when Jesus goes down into the water to take on such a load of sin! Surely it is correct to say that this act of submission to the Father's will — 'not my will, but your will be done' (Luke 22:42) — he becomes by imputation the greatest of sinners. As the sinbearer he bore all the sins of all his people (Heb. 10:14). A colossal load of guilt was laid on his back. The picture of him carrying the cross to Golgotha can be visualized as a picture of the world being carried on his back. Were he not divine it could never have been done.

The servant passages of Isaiah seem to have two main themes, the sufferings and the glories of the Messiah. Have you ever wondered where John the Baptist obtained the concept of the Lamb, 'Look, the Lamb of God, who takes away the sin of the world!' (Jn. 1:29)? Was it the Passover Lamb John was thinking of? That is possible but it is altogether more likely that he had in mind Isaiah's words, 'he was led as a lamb to the slaughter', since in the same context we have the declaration, 'and the LORD laid on him the iniquity of us all' (Is. 53:6, 7).

How appropriate that the Servant of Jehovah be buried in the waters of the Jordan and that he should rise again out of those waters — a perfect symbol of his sufferings, death and resurrection. The running waters are a fitting reminder that by his act of becoming our substitute our sins are washed away.

That this should exemplify our whole salvation is seen in the approbation of the Holy Spirit and the words of the Father. Returning to the Servant passages we read that Jehovah promised to 'put my Spirit on him' (Is. 42:1). Mark says that the heaven was 'torn open'. The world transcendent broke through. The Holy Spirit came down. The Father spoke. Here we see the Trinity: God the Father speaking, God the Son coming up out of the water, God the Holy Spirit resting upon Christ.

Why was the emblem a dove hovering over Jesus? After looking at that subject we will study the utterance of the Father at the baptism.

The heavens having been torn apart, the Holy Spirit in the form of a dove fluttered over Jesus. We recall that Noah's dove had returned to the ark with a freshly plucked olive leaf (Gen. 8:11). That was a picture of peace. A covenant of common grace in which God promised that he would never again destroy the world in a flood was about to be ushered in. Seedtime and harvest would not again be disrupted. A covenant of peace with the cosmos was about to be inaugurated. The dove was an ideal symbol of that peace.

As Jesus began his ministry officially he identified himself with his people. Here was the hand of a new race emerging from among them. While he is among them he nevertheless is marked out as the first or prototype of a new race. By him and out of him comes a new creation, the Church of the living God, his bride. The Holy Spirit hovers over him just as the Holy Spirit hovered over the waters (Gen. 1:2). In the beginning of the material world before there was symmetry and beauty, the Holy Spirit hovered in readiness over what he was about to create. In the baptism scene he hovered over Jesus. This was an evidence not only of the fact that Jesus was one with the Spirit and possessed a unique fulness of the Spirit without measure, but also that the Holy Spirit of love and peace was about to create a new creation superior by far to any physical creation, namely the creation of the Church

(Eph. 2:10). That new creation was to come out of this man, and especially out of the death and resurrection symbolized in this his baptism.

The significance of the heavens being 'torn open' which is a very vivid expression (Mk. 1:9), may be better understood when we recall the words of Jesus to Nathanael, 'I tell you the truth, you shall see heaven open, and the angels of God ascending and descending on the Son of Man' (Jn. 1:51) – and also Hebrews 10:20, where we are told that the heavenly tabernacle has now been opened for us through the body of Jesus. It is by his crucified body that the curtain of separation has been torn from top to bottom. Now all who are redeemed by that crucified body have access not into an earthly tabernacle, but into the very sanctuary of the most High in that holy world which transcends ours.

Mark, Matthew and Luke all record the voice from heaven approving the baptism, 'You are my Son, whom I love; with you I am well pleased.' Luke alone inserts the detail that Jesus was praying. 'And as he was praying, heaven was opened.' There are three occasions when the voice of the Father approves his son. The second is the transfiguration and the third was when he was teaching in Jerusalem (Matt. 17:5; Jn. 12:28). In each case we observe the Lord in a different rôle. In the first instance he is submitting to identification with his people in his baptism. Luke emphasizes the baptism as a time of prayer (Luke 3:21). This reminds us that as one of us he represents us as our priest (Heb. 5:1-5). In the transfiguration we see him as king of glory. In Jerusalem and in the temple he is revealed as teacher or prophet. The Father approves of all his work as priest, king and prophet. He loves him, is well pleased with him, and would have us hear him attentively and obediently.

This Jesus, only-begotten and beloved Son, servant in submission to a hard way; priest, king and prophet, identifies himself with all his people by immersion; an immersion which points on toward the immersion into the vortex of woe, a submersion which would save his people once and for all (Heb. 10:12).

Observe the completeness and totality of the ordinance. It is not a pouring nor is it a sprinkling. It is a burial, a baptism, a grave, a symbol of destruction, but at the same time an emergence again, a rising, a coming forth to a new age and to a new world of eternal life.

The question as to whether we are to follow our Lord in baptism is relevant. Is this expression 'follow the Lord in his baptism' correct? It is correct insofar as the ordinance is one of union or solidarity. We meet him in the one and only place where sin is dealt with and washed away, namely in the death to destruction typified in his death. That death we too must experience, not literally for that is impossible, but symbolically. The Scriptures assert the 'oneness' of Jesus' death. He died *once* and for all. We die to sin once and for all. Believer's baptism alone symbolizes that. We do not get baptized twice.

We follow the Lord in respect of testimony. He was not ashamed of his rôle as sinbearer. He was baptized publicly. We follow him in respect of open avowal of union with him.

Of course we cannot follow the Lord in the uniqueness of his baptism. He is the first one. He is the prototype. He is the one and only Lamb. His union with the Trinity was expressed in a unique way. Yet in fulfilling his command to be baptized as believers we are not only following him in dealing with the sin question (he is taking it up as sinbearer, we in being rid of it by transference), but we are also expressing union with the Trinity, for the formula in baptism is into the name of the Father, Son and Holy Spirit. Jesus is the member of the Trinity by whom our unity with the Trinity becomes a reality. These issues meet in baptism.

The testimony of the believer in his baptism

8

THINK of what it means for the new convert to be baptized! He is rejoicing in the One who has redeemed him and brought him into a new and marvellous relationship. He himself is a new creation and all things have become scintillatingly new as we sometimes sing:

> *Heaven above is softer blue,*
> *Earth below is sweeter green;*
> *something lives in every hue,*
> *Christless eyes have never seen.*[1]

The one newly born has a heart bursting with promise and thanksgiving. How does he express the forgiveness he has received? How does he tell forth the new life that is his? He has discovered the Christian community. What joy he has derived from them in counsel, guidance and help! How does he show that he is now a member of this family? Perhaps he has been a member of a Christian family and found the whole business of religion a horrible bore. Converted parents, converted sisters, services on Sunday, not allowed to indulge in sport, or go down to the recreation club! What tedium! But now there is a new song to sing. Now he realizes why it is that his family prayed so much for him and why they were so concerned about him. He can hardly find expressions adequate to extol the love of God in saving such a rebel as he. Now for the first time every word of the Psalms lights up to him. Hymns are his delight, especially verses like this which express his newly-found experience:

> *Long my imprisoned spirit lay*
> *Fast bound in sin and nature's night;*
> *Thine eye diffused a quickening ray,*
> *I woke, the dungeon flamed with light;*
> *My chains fell off, my heart was free,*
> *I rose, went forth, and followed thee.*[2]

How can the new convert enter expressively into this experience which marks his union with the Trinity, the beginning of eternal life and union with the church with all the responsibilities that entails? He reads of Timothy who made a good confession in the presence of many witnesses. Is it possible that he can do the same? This good confession had to do with eternal life to which Timothy was called (1 Tim. 6:12). 'Calling' expresses it exactly. It is by an irresistible, gracious, powerful call that conversion has taken place. Has the New Testament provided an ordinance of initiation into the church which fully tells forth the glory of this call?

Baptism answers this exactly, for a burial and resurrection vividly proclaims the whole of salvation, and gloriously so, as it is all through union with the One from whom it all comes. The new convert is laid alongside Christ in his tomb. The waters wash over him symbolizing the washing away all of his guilt. The believer is resurrected from those waters of destruction. Awaiting him is the body of believers ready to receive him and nurture him.

The provision of baptism is designed to strengthen the new believer as well as all who witness his baptism, for in itself it answers all the basic questions faced by him. We will examine these questions in a straightforward way like this:

What is a Christian?

Answer: One who is united to the Trinity through union with Christ in his death, burial and resurrection and who has had his sins washed away (Rom. 6:1-4; Col. 2:11-13; Acts 22:16).

What is a Church?

Answer: A church is an assembly of believers united to the Trinity, who have been baptized by the Holy Spirit into Christ and who now harmonize together as a body (1 Cor. 12:13 ff.; Gal. 3:26-28).

What are the privileges of church membership?

Answer: To be in union with the body of Christ local and universal; to be under preparation with them for the great Day of presentation; to be under the shepherding care of Christ's undershepherds; to be instructed by Gospel preaching and to partake of the Lord's supper (Acts 2:42; Gal. 3:26, 27; Eph. 5:25-27; Eph. 4:1-16 note especially verses 5, 11, 12).

What are the responsibilities of church membership?

Answer: Acts 2:41, 42 declares that those who repented and were baptized devoted themselves to the apostles' teaching and to the fellowship, to the breaking of bread and to prayers together.

What other responsibilities are involved in the Christian life?

Answer: Separation from the world, mortification of sin and whole-hearted service to the Lord Jesus Christ. Baptism symbolizes leaving the old world of sin behind and rising to live a new life (Rom. 6:4). Members of the body previously used in the slavery of sin are now to be used as instruments of righteousness (Rom. 6:13, 16).

How can we aim at the best possible testimony in baptism?
The emphasis on teaching which precedes baptism is clearly asserted in the great commission for to make disciples is to make pupils or learners. Because there are many implications in being baptized into the Trinity there should be careful preparation. The candidate should understand the ordinances. This is not to omit the heart and will, for baptism can be costly. It has cost some their lives, particularly in Muslim lands.

The candidate should aim at a full spiritual appreciation of the testimony involved in his baptism. If he is to be baptized with others it makes it easier because he can share the experience with them.

Both the church and the candidate should seek and pray fervently for the outpouring of the Holy Spirit upon the ordinance. To be joined to Christ is to be sealed by the Holy Spirit (Eph. 1:13; 4:30 and 2 Cor. 1:22). We should pray that the seal of assurance will be mightily strengthened through the ordinance. Furthermore, we should pray that the event will make clear impressions on the relatives and friends who witness it.

Our Lord was not ashamed to identify publicly with us in baptism. He said, 'whoever acknowledges me before men, I will acknowledge him before my Father in heaven' (Matt. 10:32). Of course, that was a reference to all occasions when it is essential for us to stand out as Christians and declare our allegiance to Christ, but it does not exclude baptism which is a very special occasion when our unity with Christ is declared.

We should feel free in the actual service, and if it is suitable for the candidate to give a few words of testimony, then that can be most appropriate. This should never be forced. Some ministers seldom encourage it since most candidates have already given a full testimony before the church.

During April 1982 the writer baptized a young man handicapped in speech and all round bodily development, one who has not been able to master reading or writing. Over a considerable period of time he maintained an excellent Christian testimony and frequently requested baptism. The elders and members of the church agreed unanimously that it would be consistent to proceed. His parents likewise agreed. When the time came to descend into the pool the young man, Stephen by name, declined until he had given testimony. I motioned to him to proceed whereupon with perfect speech he declared so that all without exception could hear, 'I believe that Jesus Christ is the Son of God, I love him and I trust him.' This proved to be the most moving part of the service. It made a deep impact on everyone, especially those who are not committed believers.

Baptism is a bodily thing, bodily not only in that the whole body is washed (Heb. 10:22), but bodily in reference to the body of Christ of which the new member now formally becomes a part, 'now you are the body of Christ, and each one of you is a part of it' (1 Cor. 12:27). The other members to whom the new convert is now being joined are all intimately involved. To the rôle played by them we now turn.

[1] George Wade Robinson, *Christian Hymns,* 654.
[2] Charles Wesley, *Christian Hymns,* 524.

The testimony of the local church in baptism

9

Being baptized by the Spirit into the body of Christ has water baptism as its sign and seal. Baptism should never be separated or isolated from the body of the church. The burden of 1 Corinthians is the unity of the church. In the introductory section Paul's appeal to them was that they had all been baptized into Christ, and not into any man such as Peter, Apollos or Paul. The Holy Spirit had done this great work and baptism in water was the symbol of it. This interpretation is consistent with similar contexts such as Galatians 3:27 ff. and Romans 6:1 ff., where the foremost truth of union of Christ with believers is linked with baptism in water which is the symbol of it.[1]

1 Corinthians 12:12-31 provides the most detailed development of the analogy of the head and body in the Scriptures. All the members have been baptized into the body. All the members are one. All are diverse. As there are different organs such as the eye, ear and hand in the human body, yet complete unity, so in the body of Christ there are different functions and different offices. As with the human body, all the parts are serving the best interests of the whole. Every additional member has to relate to the whole.

Entrance into the body is therefore very important. To allow carnal unspiritual people into membership is like grafting in malevolent cancers which will work against the healthy members and cripple the body. Cancer is seldom benign. It spreads and it destroys. The analogy of the body given in 1 Corinthians 12 is one which clearly asserts the necessity of life in all the individual members. That life is the prerequisite of the unity which Paul is urging. There is no unity between life and death, between living healthy organs and deadly cancers. Unregenerate people cannot contribute to the internal life of Christ's body. They may profit from the teaching ministry and from friendship with the members. Indeed they might by that means be cured and be born again. But if they are brought in unconverted they will be a destructive influence (2 Cor. 6:14-18).

Every person must evidence spiritual life in order to be a member of Christ's church. The procedure by which this is guaranteed is identical with the procedures of the New Testament, namely, a credible profession of repentance and faith followed by baptism and membership. The most obvious example is that of Acts chapter 2. That initial pattern is followed throughout the book of Acts. 'Repent and be baptized, *every one of you*,' said Peter (Acts 2:38). There were no exceptions to this rule.

Now it greatly confuses the issue when infants are included without repentance and faith in the hope that later they will produce repentance and faith. In order to safeguard the purity of the church those who practise infant baptism introduce confirmation exercises and services for those who, baptized as babies, later come to profess faith and express a desire to submit to church discipline and order. But no such notion of confirmation is to be found in the New Testament. It is non-existent, just as infant-baptism is non-existent. There is only one initiation exercise into the church of Christ and that is believers' baptism or, if you like, new covenant baptism. This is exclusively for those who evidence a new heart and spirit (Heb. 8:8-13). In this initiation the believer himself is exercised, as are the officers of the church, and all the members. In this chapter we consider the exercise involved for the officers of the church in preparation of candidates for baptism.

The experience of the elders of the local church
The task of the elders is to ensure that the candidate has indeed come to faith and that he understands the scope of the responsibilities that now become his as a member of Christ's body. The work of teaching is by no means confined to the expository ministry of the pulpit. The elders must ensure that the teaching is assimilated spiritually by individual members and not just intellectually. It is not difficult to give a mere assent to the Gospel. To be spiritual is to be indwelt by the Spirit and this will be evidenced in many ways such as a love for God, affection for Christians, zeal for good works, esteem for and obedience to the commands of the Bible and an ability to discern the will and mind of God in the moral law and Gospel. Fundamental, too, is the necessity of an understanding of the person and work of Christ, justification by faith, adoption by the Father and sanctification by the Spirit. After all, if the person is to be baptized into momentous union with the three persons of the Trinity then we should as a minimum expect an awareness of the respective rôles of Father, Son and the Holy Spirit in salvation.

This knowledge need not be profound or encyclopaedic, but surely we should expect it to ring true. While it is not necessary that the newly-converted be able to expound on the various doctrines of the 1689 Confession of Faith, it is advisable that he should at least know that such is subscribed to by the leaders of the church. He should also be requested to read through the church articles, which contain a summary of the truths embraced by the members. Likewise he should know the constitution in order that he is aware of his responsibilities and the order and discipline of the local church. After all, he is about to give public testimony of union with those who embrace these doctrines and practices. From the very beginning every effort should be made by him to maintain consistent and regular fellowship and prayer with the other members.

It is the business of the elders to exercise their gifts of discernment in recognizing sincerity and genuineness in the profession of faith that is made. If the candidates soon revert to unbelief and deny the profession they have made it brings the elders, the church and the Gospel into disrepute. It is the elders who are mainly responsible. They are the appointed under-shepherds. In the event of carelessness and laxity it is they who appear as goons in the eyes of the world rather than mature and discerning spiritual leaders. The keys of the kingdom of heaven (Matt. 16:19) were given to Peter to use in the exercise of discipline, that is, shutting out and closing in. That principle of discipline has not been abandoned. Discipline is an essential responsibility exercised by elders (Heb. 13:17; Acts 20:17-31). There is no way that wolves will be allowed in to destroy the flock when there are diligent and able elders exercising oversight.

The apostles were able to baptize converts quickly. This was not merely because they possessed unusual discernment, but because they were dealing with Jews or proselytes (converts to belief in the Scriptures), who were already consistent in their religious practices. For instance, most of those baptized at the time of Pentecost had travelled tremendous distances at great cost to themselves in time and money. It was their zeal for the truth that inspired them to such sacrifice. The apostles did make mistakes. This is illustrated by the case of Simon the Sorcerer (Acts 8:18, 19). The swift and severe way in which Peter dealt with Simon confirms the gravity and importance of being sure before baptism is embarked upon.

It is incumbent on the elders to explain the meaning of baptism and its relationship to the church. The basic passages which have already been expounded, such as Romans 6:1-6; Colossians 2:11-13; Acts 22:16 and 1 Peter 3:21, need to be discussed with the candidate. Further passages such as Ephesians 5:25-27 can also be opened up:

> Husbands, love your wives, just as Christ loved the church and gave himself up for her to make her holy, cleansing her by the washing with water through the word, and to present her to himself as a radiant church, without stain or wrinkle or any other blemish, but holy and blameless.

One of the practices in ancient Greece was the custom by which a bride bathed in a sacred stream before her marriage. By confession of faith and by washing of baptism Christ makes for himself a cleansed and consecrated Church free from any blemish.

An appreciation of what Christ has done for the church is the pre-eminent feature of this passage, and into this appreciation the elders should seek to lead the individual believer. Christ gave himself to the church. That is all very well, but now that church must be made ready for Christ. To this end individual members are made holy by the washing of water through the Word. The hearing of the Word has been the instrument of cleansing the believer. It is by the Word that he has been born again (Jam. 1:18; 1 Pet. 1:23). The believer now obeys, submits to, and confesses that Word. He does so in his baptism which symbolizes in a visual manner the cleansing or washing away of his sin that has already been dealt with in the spiritual realm of repentance. The Ephesians 5:25-27 passage helps to stress the corporate nature of the church, Christ's bride. The individual must be trained to think not merely of his own interests. No! He must serve the interests of the body. It is the bride that is being prepared and is made beautiful for Christ. Not self, but the church is the theme.

The exercise of the church members
When the elders are satisfied that the candidate has received the apostolic teachings (1 Jn. 4:2), has evinced a transformation of life (1 Jn. 3:9) and is in a loving relationship with the members of the church, then it is time to introduce the new member to all the other members. The way in which this is done differs in local assemblies. It is the common practice in many churches for the applicant to testify concerning his conversion and to share his experience in the hearing of the gathered body. This need not be mandatory, but if encouraged it assists all those involved to be reminded of their responsibilities with regard to 'body care' — that is, the mutual help of all the members toward each other.

An awareness of strengths and weaknesses is helpful. Where special nurture will be needed it is beneficial for the body to be alerted to this. In rare instances candidates are unable to testify before the whole church, in which case one of the elders can speak for him and answer questions from the assembly in his presence. When the whole assembly signifies satisfaction then the way is open to proceed with the baptism. This becomes an occasion in which all the members are reminded in a most vivid way of the nature of salvation and the responsibilities of walking in newness of life with all which that entails.

Thus comes to fulfilment a further instance of the great commission in which making disciples, baptizing and teaching are coordinate and complementary activities (Matt. 28:19, 20). The whole church, the elders, and the new believer, or believers, in the case of a multiple baptismal service, are involved together.

In this way, too, the aforementioned analogy of a *living* body (1 Cor. 12:12-30; Rom. 12:4-8) is maintained. The stones of a living temple are fitly joined together (Eph. 2:21, 22; 1 Pet. 2:5) and the branches of the living vine grow, being fed by the stem (Jn. 15:1-17). I have quoted the whole section of John 15:1-17 because it is there made plain that remaining in the vine is achieved by obeying the Father's commands and living a life of prayer. If a member once baptized goes back on his profession then the whole New Testament procedure of discipline must be referred to in order to maintain the purity and unity of Christ's church on earth. It is virtually impossible to maintain such discipline if a situation has come to prevail in which membership is nominal and no spiritual life of prayer, fellowship and lively service in good works has ever been expected or forthcoming. In contrast to such deadness, believers' baptism highlights the newness of life that is now a reality through union with Christ. That good work which God has begun in the believer (Phil. 1:6; Eph. 2:10), is a good work which will go from strength to strength (2 Cor. 3:18; 2 Pet. 3:18). It is a work which has been initiated by the Trinity, has been marked and sealed in baptism, and which will be consummated in the glory of the resurrection, when we shall be presented before his glorious presence without fault and with great joy.

[1] *1 Corinthians,* Leon Morris, p. 174.

The ongoing testimony of baptism

10

THE baptism of a believer is not something which is performed and then forgotten. Noah's household experienced a metaphorical baptism in the ark of Christ which we still remember (1 Pet. 3:21). We should always remember our baptism and recall to mind its implications. The ordinance possesses an ongoing testimony. By it the elders are reminded of their responsibilities. In the last chapter we considered the responsibility of the elders in preparing the candidate. In this chapter we will consider the responsibilities of nurturing the spiritual life of the one who has been baptized.

He has been raised from the dead (Eph. 2:1-10), which has been portrayed in his being raised from the waters. In a formal sense that moment marks the beginning of his life in the body of Christ, a life that requires constant nourishment, guidance and encouragement.

Separation
In baptism the convert declares before the church that he is turning his back on his old ways and abandoning them. The church is defined by Paul as those who are sanctified in Christ Jesus, which means to be set apart in Christ. Baptism illustrates that fact vividly. The separation is from the world which John defines for us in his epistle:

> Do not love the world or anything in the world. If anyone loves the world, the love of the Father is not in him. For everything in the world — the cravings of sinful man, the lust of his eyes and the boasting of what he has and does — comes not from the Father but from the world. The world and its desires pass away, but the man who does the will of God lives for ever (1 Jn. 2:15-17).

This world in its entirety is controlled by the evil one (1 Jn. 5:19). The reason for that control is because it is a world without God, a world in rebellion toward God, and a world determined to keep God out. Separation from it is by no means easy. After a while the old temptations return to the young Christian and fellow believers are needed to hold the new convert fast. From them he derives strength and courage to forsake his old habitat. Example is very important. I remember the power exerted upon me by the example of other believers when I was first converted. In them I saw visibly displayed the attributes of zeal, love and dedication. When I was baptized I truly knew my union with Christ and trusted in him. Yet in practical terms I yearned for, and required the companionship of fellow believers. I felt that I was becoming one with them. It was union with them, combined with moral support from them, more than any virtue in me, that enabled me to make a clean break and be separate from the world. The elders are always to encourage integration of the members of Christ's body in order that the strong ones will set the pace and provide a visible pattern. Integration of the new converts is essential from the beginning.

Old-fashioned separation is not popular nowadays. The churches are weaker and poorer for it. It is a delusion to think that we must be like the world to win the world. We are in the world but not of the world. The very fact that we are not dependent on the broken cisterns of the world, but derive a fulness of joy and satisfaction from Christ our head, is the strength of our witness and the star attraction used by the Holy Spirit to draw others (Jer. 2:13; Jn. 7:28; 10:10).

The Old Testament paradigm for separation is the exodus of the children of Israel from Egypt. All were baptized into Moses in the cloud and in the sea (1 Cor. 10:1 ff.). The sea was a sea of destruction, and the cloud a cloud of protection. By the one they were saved from the other.

The drama was unforgettable. It was the supreme enactment of salvation just as believers' baptism is. Yet afterwards many turned back in their hearts to Egypt. The danger of going back as they did is a real danger (Heb. 3:7-19; 1 Cor. 10:6-13). Separation is not enough. There must be incorporation into the body. Salvation is from darkness to light, from Satan to God, from the family of the world to the family of the Father of light (Acts 26:18). The idea of nationhood became clear to those Israelites, but the idea of a closely-knit spiritual family is a New Testament reality to which we now turn.

Adoption
Baptism in the name of the Father and of the Son and of the Holy Spirit reminds us of the relationship that each believer sustains to the persons of the Godhead. Union with Christ is the foundation. He is the head and we are the members. Every major analogy used to illustrate the nature of the church of Christ in the New Testament stresses the union of all the members with their head (Jn. 15:1-12; Rom. 12:1-8; 1 Cor. 12:12 ff.; Eph. 4:1-16; Col. 2:18, 19). The relationship we sustain to the Father arises out of our union

with Christ. This is beautifully portrayed in the letter to the Hebrews:

> In bringing many sons to glory, it was fitting that God, for whom and through whom everything exists, should make the Pioneer of their salvation perfect through suffering. Both the one who makes men holy and those who are made holy are of the same family. So Jesus is not ashamed to call them brothers. He says, 'I will declare your name to my brothers; in the presence of the congregation I will sing your praises.' And again, 'I will put my trust in him.' And again he says, 'Here am I, and the children of God has given me' (Heb. 2:10-13).

The rôle of Christ is clearly stated as his objective, namely, bringing many sons to glory and making them holy in the process. His rôle was the rôle of saviourhood which involved suffering. Note the descriptions of those whom he redeems: 'sons of glory', 'members of a holy family', 'brothers of Christ', 'children of God'. Christ is exulting and rejoicing in the relationship which he, together with his people, sustain to the Father. 'You are all sons of God through faith in Christ Jesus' (Gal. 3:26). 'Because you are sons, God sent the Spirit of his Son into our hearts, the Spirit who calls out, "Abba, Father"' (Gal. 4:6). 'The Spirit himself testifies with our spirit that we are God's children. Now if we are children, then we are heirs — heirs of God and co-heirs with Christ, if indeed we share in his sufferings in order that we may also share in his glory' (Rom. 8:16, 17).

The implications of this new relationship of adoption are enormous. Into union with the Father the convert has been baptized. There are new family relationships, new family responsibilities, a new family code of conduct, a new family freedom which must be understood and not abused — even a new family language, the spiritual language of Zion the Church. The latter is very soon learned and need not be taught, but all the other aspects require leadership and tuition.

For instance, the new convert may come from a respectable middle-class background in which there are fixed prejudices about other groups of people or other nationalities. In one sentence the apostle Paul joins together groups that have been worlds apart. Baptism represents our being joined to a head who is the head of a body of all tribes, peoples, languages and nationalities. In this body there is no longer Jew or Greek, slave or free, male or female, for we are all one in Christ Jesus (Gal. 3:28). A white South African has to learn to have a completely different attitude toward black Christians. Likewise black converts who have inherited terrific bitterness toward the whites, because of their superior ugly attitudes and exploitation, now have the formidable task of learning to view white believers as brothers in Christ.

In Muslim countries the gulf between males and females is enormous. To accept the truth that Christ has liberated women and given them equality in their access to God the Father is something not easily achieved. Other fac-

56

tors enter in which also require tuition, such as Biblical submission of wives to husbands, children to parents, employees to employers, younger men to older, younger women to older ones and members to elders. Ephesians 5:22-6:9; 1 Peter 5:1-5, and 1 Timothy 5:1-19, are three examples of detailed teaching on inter-relationships. We are all in the same family, but there are many different functions (Rom. 12:4-8). These functions have to be noted and the new believer has to adjust himself to them.

Especially important is the new code of conduct. Now that we are all sons and daughters by virtue of our union with Christ by faith, how are we to behave in the family? As God's chosen people holy and dearly loved we have this code of conduct:

> Therefore, as God's chosen people, holy and dearly loved, clothe yourselves with compassion, kindness, humility, gentleness and patience. Bear with each other and forgive whatever grievances you may have against one another. Forgive as the Lord forgave you. And over all these virtues put on love, which binds them all together in perfect unity. Let the peace of Christ rule in your hearts, since as members of one body you were called to peace. And be thankful (Col. 3:12-15).

The radical freedom into which the new family members come has also to be adjusted to. This freedom is radical because salvation in no way depends on duties performed. Not by any deeds done or laws kept are we saved. Yet paradoxically we are more concerned than ever the Pharisees were to please God by what we do. Good works are our daily concern. Yet these works are always performed out of love and gratitude, never out of servile fear or through the false idea that we can earn God's favour by them.

We are preoccupied with knowing the mind of God. His laws and commandments are precious to us. He requires that we love him with all our hearts and our neighbours as ourselves. The practical implications of this love are reflected in the ten commandments. The spiritual requirements of those commandments are staggering because we are required to strive after perfection in thought, word and deed. Our Lord's exposition of the commandments in the Sermon on the Mount make this plain (Matt. 5:17-48). The new member of God's family soon discovers that while he delights in God's law as holy, just and good, he finds another law working in him which hinders him. This leads us to mortification of sin, a painful but essential area in every Christian's life. Especially does the new convert need teaching in this department.

Mortification
From the very beginning the difference between definitive sanctification and progressive sanctification needs to be instilled into the new convert. Definitive sanctification is that setting apart of the believer for God once and for all. Nothing expresses that more fully or satisfactorily than baptism. Ris-

ing from the water all sin has been washed away. 'But you were washed, you were sanctified, you were justified' (1 Cor. 6:11). All our work must be based on justification by faith. We have been justified. We must not go back to build that foundation. The guilt of *all* sin has been disposed of. But what about remaining or indwelling sin?

The 1689 Confession declares that, 'those who are united to Christ, effectually called, and regenerated, have a new heart and a new spirit created in them; and by his Word and Spirit dwelling within them, this personal work of sanctification is indeed carried further.' It then goes on to say that 'Sin's mastery over them is completely broken,' 'evil desires increasingly weakened,' and 'saving graces increasingly enlivened and strengthened.' The clause, 'Sin's mastery over them is completely broken,' is easier said or written than experienced. It comes as a shock to new believers to find that sin's corrupt remnants give rise to a continued warfare. Indeed for a time sin's corrupt remnants may gain the upper hand.

Perhaps no writer has described the vicious nature of remaining sin in the believer better than John Owen. 'Sin,' he declares, 'will not only be striving, acting, rebelling, troubling, disquieting, but if let alone, if not continually mortified, it will *bring forth great, cursed, scandalous, soul-destroying sins.'* He quotes Galatians 5:19-21 which outlines the works of the flesh such as adultery, idolatry, hatred, heresies and drunkenness, and reminds us of David and the disastrous course of sin which he took as a believer. Owen describes sin as a monster which always aims at the utmost: 'every unclean thought or glance would be adultery if it could; every covetous desire would be oppression, every thought of unbelief would be atheism, might it grow to its head.'[1] Sin proceeds to its height by degrees. It is exceedingly deceitful because it would deceive by pretending sin is not so bad, when in fact, its only and ultimate aim and end is death (Jam. 1:13-15).

Nothing but mortification can prevent sin from growing in the heart and devastating the life of the believer. Mortification is the only way. Sin must be withered at its root every hour. Such discipline requires great will and determination. It can only be done through the Holy Spirit, as it says in Romans 8:13, 'if you live according to the sinful nature, you will die; but by the Spirit you put to death the misdeeds of the body, you will live.'

It is fatal to leave the young convert to himself. The implications of the new life he has received in Christ, exemplified in his baptism, should be explained to him. As the days lengthen to months and the months to years he needs tutoring, guidance and pastoral care.

Transformation
We have thought of the power of indwelling sin (limitless if not mortified), but now turn our attention to the strengthening of the new man and to

those graces within him, by which the constant demands of sin might be crucified and conquered.

Transformation is by the renewing of the mind (Rom. 12:2). This involves the reception and understanding of the teachings of Scripture. The context of the Romans 12:2 passage shows that this knowledge is entirely different in its character from other disciplines that are learned such as mathematics, physics, history and geography. It is a knowledge indissolubly linked or wedded to practice for it says, 'Then you will be able to test and approve what God's will is.' It is related to our thought processes, our speech and to all our personal relationships at home, at work and in the church. According to Peter it is a 'growing, gracious' knowledge. 'But grow in the grace and knowledge of our Lord and Saviour Jesus Christ' (2 Pet. 3:18). Apart from the work of the Holy Spirit graciously imparting and applying this knowledge there can be no useful progress whatsoever (1 Cor. 2:1-16).

Moreover, the knowledge imparted by the Holy Spirit through the Scriptures is a knowledge which is related to other members of the body of Christ. In its practical outworking each member grows in his relationship with the other members (Eph. 4:15, 16). 'Each member belongs to all the others' (Rom. 12:5). The church is the guardian of the truth (1 Tim. 3:15), and the members are all trained for works of service through the ministry of the church. All the members have to learn how to function within the church and how to apply the spiritual knowledge they receive. Every newborn Christian should be subject to a shepherding and teaching ministry, so that he will not be blown about by every wind of doctrine, but develop in maturity and learn to have a sober assessment of his own function and place in the body (Eph. 4:11-16; Rom. 12:3).

Believer's baptism symbolizes the transformation we have been considering, the putting off of the old and the putting on of the new. The transformation which is involved is begun when the believer is united to Christ, and this continues all his life (2 Cor. 7:1). The responsibility of the elders is to make all this plain. Hence Paul could write and say, 'you were taught – to be made new in the attitude of your minds' (Eph. 4:22, 23).

Beautification
Transformation involves a change from one state into another. The old was ugly: the new is beautiful. The old way was hideous like the great red dragon (Rev. 12:3); the new way is beautiful like the city of peace (Rev. 21:2). Transformation is into the likeness of Christ:

And we, who with unveiled faces all reflect the Lord's glory, are being transformed into his likeness with ever-increasing glory, which comes from the Lord, who is the Spirit (2 Cor. 3:18).

The life of Christ in this world was glorious. 'We have seen his glory,' said John, 'the glory of the Son, full of grace and truth' (Jn. 1:14). Jesus described some of the graces that characterize the Christian, such as meekness, purity and peace (Matt. 5:1-11). The church as a whole is predestinated to be made beautiful, that is to be conformed to Christ (Rom. 8:29; Rev. 21:2). Beautiful character is of the utmost importance. It must be described, taught and urged from the very beginning of a Christian's experience (Col. 3:12-17).

Evangelism
In most cases a person converted and baptized has the opportunity to witness to his or her own circle of relatives and friends. This witness consists both of life and words. Others see the change and hear in words the explanation of the convert. If there is no satisfactory change of life behind these words then there is no value in the testimony. The elders should make sure that a testimony is sincere and consistent.

Even when the preaching under which a person has been converted is powerful and Biblical the new convert still retains much of his old thinking. For instance, he is likely to attribute to unbelievers powers that they do not possess and think that their choice of God is the basis of salvation. There is always the tendency to think that natural men seek truth and all that is needed is some correction, rather than realizing that natural men are at enmity to God and regeneration is imperative (Rom. 8:7; Jn. 3:3).

Teaching of truth comes mainly by the ministry of the pulpit, but personal application is very important. Wrong presuppositions and attitudes require early, gentle and wise correction.

The more beautiful, holy, prayerful, loving and mature a church is, the more powerful will the evangelism of that assembly be.

Too often we have thought in terms of organization and efficiency as tantamount to effective evangelism. Our Lord prayed for unity among his people, 'that the world might believe' (Jn. 17:21-23). Unity and love in a church are potent factors used by the Holy Spirit to draw outsiders. If a new convert is brought early into the realization and appreciation of these factors it means that his spiritual usefulness and potential will be developed early to the advantage of all. How happy is that convert who is used by the Holy Spirit in a powerful way to draw others. Like that woman in Samaria who went to call all her friends, the new convert has the opportunity and enthusiasm to invite others. Awareness of these factors by elders and church members is most helpful. Baptism is an ordinance designed for the edification of the local church, but the overflow of the blessings involved, and the ever-present prospect and possibility of bringing in outsiders should never be overlooked, and certainly never despised.

[1] *Works* vol. 6, p. 12.

The testimony of baptism to the new covenant

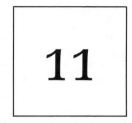

11

In baptism the blessings of the new covenant are ratified and sealed to the believer in the presence of the church. The substance of the new covenant is that God will write his laws in the minds of his people. By this means they will all know him intimately and personally. Hence they will be his people and he will be their God. They are just and right in his sight for their sins are forgiven. Baptism is a high point, a major occasion in the life of a believer, a time never to be forgotten. Can there be anything greater or more important for a human being than the reality of unity with the Trinity?

The completeness of the blessings of the new covenant is expressed in the Trinitarian statement, 'I immerse you into the name of the Father and the Son and the Holy Spirit.' As has been demonstrated, a fulness or completeness of union is signified, a fulness of love and intimacy. By the new covenant, then, we receive the Father, the Son and the Holy Spirit, together with the privileges which come with this gracious union with the Trinity.

1. The Father
The very nature of heaven is expressed in the promise and fulfilment of the New Covenant: 'I will be their God' (Jer. 31:33; Heb. 8:10; Rev. 21:3). In what way will he be their God? He will be their God by proving to them his immeasurable love. The awful condition in which they were found is illustrated by Ezekiel when he describes vividly a newly born infant discarded in an open field and dying in its blood, its cord uncut. Abandoned as worthless, it is perishing. This is a picture of original sin (Ezek. 16:1-5; Ps. 51:5). When his people deserved nothing but wrath and eternal damnation he demonstrated his wonderful love to them by taking them up, by washing them, and making them clean. He has proved his endearment to them by changing their wicked hearts and by transforming them into his own dear children. By adopting them into his family he proves himself to be a loving Father to them. Even though they may have a history of appalling unfaithfulness he

now establishes an everlasting covenant with them in which their hearts are bound to his (Ez. 16:60). He will show his love for them by working all things for their good (Rom. 8:28).

The sixteenth chapter of Ezekiel referred to above describes powerfully the history of God's covenant dealings. When the old covenant broke down he abrogated it. He then made a new one the essence of which is the new birth: a new heart and a new spirit (Ez. 16:60; Jer. 31:33-34). The old covenant embraced all the members of the Hebrew nation whether they were born again or not; the new covenant embraces a new nation consisting of all kinds of people from different races, languages and cultures, but they all have one essential characteristic in common. They all know God because they have all been called, born again, adopted, each one into the family, God himself declares, 'they will all know me, from the least of them to the greatest' (Jer. 31:34).

To know the Father is to know his love immeasurable. Expressions of this love can be seen in the Father working all things for the good of his children (Rom. 8:28). This love is observed too in his being to his people their Friend, their Portion, their Sun and their Shield.

A true friend is one with whom you can share, one who can be trusted at all times and who is always loyal — one who will never betray you. Such is the Father who is also our Portion, which is another way of saying he is our possession. The splendour, beauty, delights, wisdom, and riches of his creation he shares with us. Especially is this true of his new creation which we will possess and enjoy; we will appreciate the attributes of our Father as they relate to the creation of a new heaven and a new earth. The error of fallen mankind is to seek enjoyment of the present creation to the exclusion of the Creator.

The sun is a world of light and warmth to us. So is our Father a spiritual light to us. We walk in the light he has given to us and in the new world to come he will be the light so we will have no more need of the sun.

Not only is our Father, our Friend, our Portion, our Sun — he is also our Shield. We have to endure many dangers and hazards in a perpetual conflict as we live the life of faith in a sinful world. But our relationship with our Father, and the love he bears to us, guarantees protection in the battle. 'He who fears the LORD has a secure fortress, and for his children it will be a refuge' (Prov. 14:26). When wounded or weak he knows our state and remembers that we are dust (Ps. 103:14). When missiles that we do not detect are hurled against us he will be our shield.

All this our Father is to us by the new covenant which is everlasting. Unlike the old covenant it can never be broken. When he created us in Christ he wrote his laws in our hearts. He began a good work in us which he will complete (Phil. 1:8). In the accomplishment of that good work we must not omit the truth that he is faithful in correcting and chastising us. Such chatisement is a further proof that we are loved by him. It is an important proof of our adoption.

2. *The Son*

We are observing the nature and blessing of the new covenant in which all believers know God, from the least of them to the greatest of them. We have seen the love of the Father in this covenant. Supremely is his love demonstrated in providing his Son as the mediator of a new and better covenant (Heb. 8:64 ff.). Stupendous is that love which gave his Son even to the death of the Cross in order that our sins might be covered. Not only is astonishing love displayed but in providing a perfect man we see the wisdom of the Father. Paul declares this wisdom in writing to the Corinthians. When all the wise men, and all the brilliant philosophers of this world, failed miserably to produce any solution for a dying race of men, God presented his superlative wisdom. This was to unite a people to Christ. Through that union 'Christ Jesus has become for us wisdom from God — that is, our righteousness, holiness and redemption' (1 Cor. 1:30). We will look briefly at the meaning of these three words because they sum up the blessings of the new covenant as they are mediated to us through Christ. In observing the fulness of the provision we see exemplified and displayed the wisdom of God, in contrast to the emptiness of the world's wisdom.

(i) RIGHTEOUSNESS. In the new covenant God says he will be our God and will remember our sins no more. The reason is not because he has laid aside his justice but rather because Christ in his death and sufferings has met all that justice can require. His sufferings were comprehensive and satisfied all the stringent demands of the law.

Union with him means his perfect life is imputed to us. Hence he is called 'the LORD our Righteousness' (Jer. 23:6). Union in his death means that God cannot punish us a second time. We have been crucified with Christ (Gal. 2:20). We cannot be crucified a second time.

Now we are right in the sight of the holy God, justified before him because of our union with Christ. All defilement and guilt have been removed by Christ's death in our place on the Cross. Not only so, but the perfect life lived by Christ our Head is ours by imputation being put on us and around us as our very own righteousness (Jer. 23:6). It is like wearing daily the coat of many colours which Jacob gave to his son Joseph whom he favoured and loved. It was a constant reminder to Jacob of his son. So by wearing the robe of Christ's righteousness our Father sees all the colours and merits of Christ's perfect life lived for us.

(ii) HOLINESS. We are observing the wisdom of God in the provision of our every need in the person of Christ to whom we are joined in baptism. Through union with Christ a further essential factor in our salvation is provided. This is holiness. The first imperative is justification, forgiveness and acceptance. That is why justification by faith is the first article of the Christian faith. On that foundation we then proceed to the next necessity — a holy life, for without holiness no man will see the Lord (Heb. 12:14). In the New Testament the words 'holiness' and 'sanctification' are synonymous. To sanctify in the first place means to set apart, and secondly it means to make holy. About half the references point to initial sanctification, which means to set apart. When we believed we were perfectly sanctified in the sense that we were set apart in Christ once and for all. The use of the past tense reminds us of this fact. You were idolaters, slanderers, swindlers — *but you have been sanctified* (1 Cor. 6:11).

Now, having been set apart, we are made holy in the progressive sense. It is like an old ramshackle house. First it is bought, then it is systematically renovated. Bunyan uses the illustration of a fortified city. First it is conquered. Then it is systematically subdued. Christ is the centre of power from which all the means of our being made holy proceed. As the head of the body with which he is united he provides the pastors and teachers (Eph. 4:11). He prays for his own and safeguards them continually (Heb. 7:25).

(iii) REDEMPTION. The final stage of our salvation is the redemption of our bodies. This too is brought about through our union with Christ. Having bought us (to redeem means to buy) he will not leave us in a condition of humiliation. As the king exalted to whom all power is given he will raise our bodies from the dust in the last day. Thereafter we will always enjoy his company.

In this way of union the Father has shown his wisdom in making Christ all that we need, righteousness (justification), holiness (sanctification) and redemption.

When we are joined to Christ we find in him all that is needed.

3. The Holy Spirit
In the new covenant God makes over to us himself, his Son and the person of the Holy Spirit. This granting or giving of himself could not be more personal or intimate than it is. He is not a God afar off but near. He is *our* God. We are *his* people. This is the heart of the new agreement or covenant. Therefore unity with the Trinity is a very suitable expression. To be plunged into Christ in baptism is not irreverent. A total union or identification of that nature is necessary. Our fall into sin was terrible, as was Christ's death to retrieve us.

It is equally fitting that we should be plunged into the Father and the Spirit. We have seen that without reservation the Father is one with his adopted children. He is not ashamed of that relationship of union.

John the Baptist promised that Christ would baptize with the Holy Ghost. Our Lord confirmed that he would do this and designated Pentecost as the time. That event proved Christ to be Lord and proved too that the Church was the creation and possession of the Holy Spirit. As we have seen baptism signifies that something is complete, a once and for all event. When we are savingly joined to Christ that is something which is a decisive once and for all event. Likewise when the Holy Spirit came upon the apostolic church at Pentecost it was a baptism, that word signifying a once and for all unrepeatable event. That was a day of birth. Thereafter he came upon the Samaritans (Acts 8), and the Gentiles at Caesarea (Acts 11), and the Ephesians (Acts 19), as proof that they too were purified by faith (Acts 15:9).

From the time of Pentecost onward the Holy Spirit applies the finished work of Christ to all his people. The work of the Holy Spirit is also accomplished on the basis of unity. The first and greatest work of the Spirit is to regenerate sinners. From the moment of regeneration or new birth onward the Holy Spirit indwells the believer. To indwell a person is to be united to that person.

Various expressions are used to describe the operations of the Holy Spirit in God's people. When he regenerates them he seals them with a seal of assurance. From that time onward his very presence in them is the guarantee that he will complete his work (2 Cor. 1:22).

When he regenerates them he anoints them or opens their eyes to see the glory and virtues of Christ (2 Cor. 1:21; 1 Jn. 2:27). That work of anointing or teaching is carried forward as the Holy Spirit gives an ability to understand the Scriptures.

By indwelling them, teaching them, assuring them, correcting them and enabling them, the Holy Spirit carries on to completion his great work of preparing and perfecting the redeemed of Christ for the glorious kingdom which is their inheritance.

4. The Privileges of the New Covenant
Union with the Trinity is in itself an inestimable privilege. When we read in Revelation of the new Jerusalem, the new earth and heavens, we see that the first enjoyment of the eternal state is not the glory of those mansions, or the golden streets, the river or the trees or even the inhabitants, but God himself. God himself will be with them (Rev. 21:3). Their chief pleasure will be the knowledge and service of the Father, the presence and sight of Christ and the indwelling presence of the Holy Spirit.

The gifts of the eternal God are gifts which reflect his glory. As we progress in our understanding we appreciate more the priceless value of the very first gift we received. 'I will give you a new heart and put a new spirit in you' (Ez. 36:26).

This new heart consists of a disposition to love God and his laws. Those laws are written on the heart. What a very great change it is to have the old depraved heart of enmity removed and replaced with a heart that desires to obey, and which sees God's laws as holy, just and good, laws in which to delight.

With this primary gift of the new covenant which is inward come other blessings which are outward, such as a new spiritual family; fathers, mothers, brothers, sisters, a hundredfold. Not only is sweet fellowship within the church known by us on earth, but we can look forward to meeting God's household from every age: Abel, Enoch, Noah, Abraham, Moses, David, Isaiah, Daniel, the apostles, and all the Christians of the last days.

Guaranteed too in the covenant is the grace of God to persevere to the end. Part of our privilege is the correction and chastisement necessary for our growing in grace. Yet whatever pain there is we know that our loving heavenly Father will never abandon that great work he has begun in us. Having loved us from before the foundation of the world and having brought us into the new covenant relationship, he will never leave us nor forsake us. Such are our privileges.

How to enter into the new covenant
'Come to me,' declares the Lord, 'and I will make an everlasting covenant with you' (Is. 55:3). This cannot be the old agreement or covenant made with Israel because that has passed away. This new agreement is everlasting. It is made by God and therefore cannot be broken. How do we enter into such a union?

Let us look at the instructions. We are urged not to spend our energies on procuring things which can never satisfy our souls. Rather, in our thirst for fulfilment and satisfaction we must go to the source of living waters. This can only be found in the One who stood up in the temple courts of Jerusalem and made a general invitation, with a loud voice so that all could hear, 'if a man is thirsty, let him come to me and drink. Whoever believes in me, as the Scripture has said, streams of living water will flow from within him' (Jn. 7:37, 38).

In order to come to this Saviour we are instructed to hear or listen intently in order that we can understand the nature of the good news. Note the emphasis given to hearing, because faith comes by hearing: 'Listen, listen to me,' says the prophet, 'and eat what is good, and your soul shall delight itself in the richest of fare. *Give ear* and come to me; *hear me,* that your soul may live. I will make an everlasting covenant with you' (Is. 55:2, 3).

In listening to the instructions we note three essentials: 1. Wickedness must be forsaken, 2. The guilt incurred by that wickedness can all be forgiven, 3. There is nothing meritorious that we can contribute ourselves.

Following these three points one by one we note, firstly, that in seeking the Lord while he may be found and in calling on him while he is near the wicked man must forsake his ungodly manner of life and his evil thoughts. Secondly, in doing this he will find mercy and pardon, because Christ 'was pierced for our transgressions' (Is. 53:5). Thirdly, he must not attempt to rely upon his own righteousness in any way. In other words, he must come 'without money' (Is. 55:1).

The mistake which destroys more people than does any other is the notion that human goodness apart from Christ can please God. *All* our righteousness is as filthy rags. We must come as we are and not try first to make ourselves a bit better. In forsaking all our own righteousness we must trust only in what has been provided for us. Looking only to Christ we will see in him everything we need. All we have to do is to receive the gift of eternal life which he has procured for all who come to him.

In this simple way we will come to enjoy all the benefits of an everlasting, unbreakable agreement achieved through union with the Father, Son and Holy Spirit.

'Come and I will make an everlasting covenant with you.'

Suggested Reading
One of the Puritan divines, Richard Alleine (1611-1681), wrote a treatise with the title, *Heaven Opened* and subtitle, 'The Riches of God's Covenant Grace' (Baker and Summit Books, 360 pp, paperback, £2.20 from E.P.). Alleines thesis runs as follows: God has in his covenant made over to us, 1. Himself, 2. His Son, 3. His Spirit, 4. The earth, 5. The angels of light, 6. The powers of darkness, 7. Death, 8. The Kingdom, 9. All the means of salvation. By numbers 6 and 7 he means that we have been given victory over the powers of darkness and victory over the grave.

The testimony of baptism for procrastinators and sick people

12

THE first person I ever baptized was a man who had been a Christian for 40 years. What had held him back? It was a lack of assurance. He believed that he had to attain a full measure of assurance to qualify. Although a devout and earnest believer he did not understand that repentance and faith alone should decide the issue.

There are a variety of reasons why some sincere Christians have not come forward for baptism. Some have not been baptized as believers because they are not sure whether their baptism as infants is valid or not. Even when they come to see that baptism is essentially for believers and must by its very nature be based on faith, they feel that they have delayed for so long that the issue is no longer relevant. That is a grave mistake, for the initiation ordained by Christ is of paramount importance. If the Lord came to you personally and commanded you to perform an act of obedience would you argue with him and say that you knew a better way? Or would you say that his command was nullified because neglect of it had gone on so long that now it no longer retained its validity?

Someone may argue that the ordinance is important for beginners, but once maturity is gained the basic lessons of baptism are no longer relevant. To this reasoning we point to the chapters which describe the place of the elders and the local church in the ordinance. As the celebration of the Lord's Table is no private affair but essentially something for the body, so baptism involves the local church. It may be argued that the Ethiopian eunuch was alone with Philip when baptized. But his case was exceptional. He was alone on a journey home and we have nothing to prove that the Christian Church was yet established in his native land. A chancellor of the exchequer does not travel alone. There must surely have been a company of colleagues who accompanied him. Nevertheless such companions could hardly form a congregation. Despite this, the Church to the end of the age will benefit from the account of his baptism in Acts chapter 8.

We have already shown that the church shares in the spiritual experience of every new member and that every baptism should remind the entire assembly of the nature of discipleship: separation, adoption, mortification, transformation and beautification (see chapter 9). All the members are corporately involved. All the members deserve and expect that each individual should follow Christ's instructions in order that the benefits of the ordinance be shared. When we witnessed the baptism of the brother who had delayed for forty years, our joy in his experience was great as we contemplated and appreciated his union with Christ and ourselves. We were sorry that he had not come forward earlier, but apart from that our joy was undiminished. Our enjoyment of union with him continues to this time.

No! Delay does not invalidate the obligation of obedience to Christ's command. but what are we to say to those who have been sprinkled as believers but not immersed? And while dealing with the subject of inadequate or partial baptism, what about a person who was immersed as a Mormon, or on a basis which was not truly Christian? What then?

The example of Paul recorded in Acts 19 helps us to answer these questions. Paul came across twelve disciples who had been immersed on the basis of John's baptism but not in the name of the Trinity. The apostle promptly proceeded to rectify this shortcoming and fulfilled the commission of our Lord. We should act along the same lines. If a person has been baptized as a Jehovah's Witness or Mormon that baptism is in no way valid because of the totally heretical nature of those sects, particularly in view of their defective views of the Trinity. Such a person needs to tell forth the truth of his or her conversion in proper believers' baptism in the name of the Trinity. If John's baptism was half-way to the truth yet still regarded as inadequate by Paul how much more is the baptism of a false cult inadequate?

What, then, of the person who has been sprinkled as a believer but not immersed? He has begun on right lines. We gladly acknowledge that he has testified to the fact of his repentance and faith. The basis of his baptism, namely faith in Christ and the Trinity, has been declared, but the mode is incomplete and therefore defective. He needs to complete what has begun. Union with Christ has not been demonstrated. It should be, for the sake of obedience to the truth, and for the sake of the church. In completing the ordinance by obedience to the correct mode, the nature of the case can be explained to the congregation.

Some may object to this on the basis that it is legalistic to bother about details, such as mode, but we should remember that our Lord spared no pains to live a perfect life for us, and in his death endured all the pain that was our due. Surely we can fulfil properly the very few tiny and painless obligations which he laid upon us in his parting instructions. In Old Testament times enormous amounts of precision and obligation were required of God's people. Now we have but two ordinances, and the inconvenience involved in the fulfilment of them is absolutely minimal. In the chapter 'What constitutes a valid baptism', this is discussed in more detail.

The recognition of a credible testimony

13

NOBODY could be left in any doubt that the gift of the Holy Spirit was given at Pentecost. The result of this was that every person who believed and was baptized could be assured of the gift of the person and work of the Spirit (Acts 2:38, 39). Every person baptized by the Spirit was baptized into the body of Christ. The baptism in water which followed repentance and faith was a symbol of what already had happened to the convert: he had been baptized into Christ's body (1 Cor. 12:13).

The New Testament knows of no exceptions to this rule either in its examples or in its language.

A difficulty could be helpfully removed from the minds of some by explaining that it is not necessary that every believer receive visible and audible proof that they are the recipients of the gift of the Holy Spirit. It was necessary at the beginning as a decisive confirmation of the inauguration of the new and final age — the Messianic era. But even then we must recognise that the extraordinary and supernatural phenomenon is reported on only four occasions. Nothing is said in all the other cases. The 120 experienced tongues of flame, but not the 3,000 that were subsequently converted.

To circumvent doubt or division, audible and visible proof was given. This was to prove the Gentiles were included in the same body by the same gift of the person and work of the Holy Spirit (Acts 15:8,9). This gift was confirmed by the laying on of the apostles' hands (something unique to them) in Samaria (Acts 8), Caesarea (Acts 9-11), and later at Ephesus (Acts 19). Subsequent to the establishment of the Christian Church it was no longer necessary to furnish visible (tongues of fire) and audible (tongues and prophecies) proof that we have the gift of the Spirit. The new birth is our proof. By the Holy Spirit we have been baptised into Christ (Gal. 3:25-27; 1 Cor. 12:12ff.), have been anointed (2 Cor. 1:21; 1 Jn. 2:27) and sealed (Eph. 1:13, 4.30; 2 Cor.

1:22). We have holiness of life given to us by the Spirit as well as fruitfulness, comfort, knowledge, the ability to pray in the Spirit, assurance, and guidance. These are proofs that we have received the Holy Spirit. To receive Christ is to receive the Holy Spirit (Rom. 8:9). Nowhere are we commanded, still less required, to produce special supernatural signs that we have the Holy Spirit. Our proof that we are indwelt by the Holy Spirit is that we constantly bear his fruit (Gal. 5:22ff.), enjoy his seal of assurance (2 Cor. 1:22), pray by his help (Rom. 8:26), have been taught by him (1 Jn. 2:27), receive his guidance and comfort (Jn. 14:26; Rom. 8:14), are being transformed by him (2 Cor. 3:18), and above all, have been born again through him, and by him have been made into new creatures in Christ (2 Cor. 5:17). We know we live in the Father and in the Son by the Holy Spirit who has been given to us (1 Jn. 3:24). A person may do many wonderful things in the name of Christ; yet if he does not have the fruit of the Spirit he will be cast into hell as Jesus said:

> Not everyone who says to me, 'Lord, Lord', will enter the kingdom of heaven, but only he who does the will of my Father who is in heaven. Many will say to me on that day, 'Lord, Lord, did we not prophesy in your name, and in your name drive out demons and perform many miracles?' Then I will tell them plainly, 'I never knew you. Away from me, you evildoers!' (Matt. 7:21-23).

Explanation concerning a credible profession of faith is appropriate because of those who are suspicious of this subject. They object to it on the grounds that it is too subjective, that is, that we have no right to pry into individual religious experiences. Yet I maintain that it is not a thing indecent, improper or unkind to set about the work of recognising a credible profession of faith. If we are unable to recognise our fellow believers, who are our own spiritual brothers and sisters, then we are in a sad state indeed! Christians are required to recognise elders and deacons according to principles laid down in 1 Timothy 3 and Titus 1. In a previous exposition we saw how the elders and the members combine in recognising new believers. Discernment of spiritual matters is never perfect or infallible, but that in no way removes the responsibility of discerning what is a credible profession and what may be deemed otherwise.

How do we go about this matter? A brief reminder of some of the New Testament epistles will help us both in self-examination and in reminding us of the main features of a Christian.

According to *Romans* a Christian is one who repents of sin and trusts only and wholly in the imputed righteousness of Christ for salvation. He is justified by faith and shows the fruits of that justification (5:1-9). He is engaged in the battle to mortify all sin (chapters 6, 7). He evidences that he has the Holy Spirit indwelling his life and rejoices in the great doctrines of sovereign grace (chapter 8). He submits to the practical teachings about the church and submission to civil authorities (chapters 12, 13). He is ready to live in such a way as not to offend weaker brethren (chapters 14, 15).

According to *James* faith must be accomplished by good works, otherwise it is false and hypocritical (2:18). A true Christian is one who is not 'in it' just for himself. He must show willingness to visit the fatherless and widows in their affliction (1:27). Moreover, he must show that at least he has begun in the difficult task of taming the tongue (chapter 3).

A scholar by the name of Bornemann has advanced the thesis that 1 Peter was originally a baptismal sermon in loose association with Psalm 34.[1] A Christian according to Peter's first letter, is one who has been saved by baptism (3:21). This baptism, of course, represents a baptism into Christ by which the believer has been born again, and by which new life he has joy inexpressible, even in trials, because he knows he is receiving the goal of his faith even the salvation of his soul (1:1-9). He is concerned to purify himself through obedience to the truth (1:22). He submits himself to rulers and masters because he has embraced the Shepherd of his soul (2:13-25). Marriage is held in honour by the believer, and no person's profession of faith can be acceptable who lives in immorality or sin (3:1-7). The elements of submission and obedience must be present in a person who professes faith. There must be a teachable spirit. No lawless person can be accepted no matter how eloquent he or she may be with the mouth (5:1-6).

According to the *Hebrews* epistle the Christian is one who holds to Christ in faith and obedience — that is, to Christ as king, prophet and priest. He proves this faith by his willingness to meet with Christians and by taking an interest in them (10:25). He shows some (even if it is a little) endurance in bearing hardship, because discipline is an essential part of the Christian life. Without discipline we cannot be true sons and daughters (12:4-13). A further mark of a credible profession is submission to the oversight of the local church (13:17).

According to *Ephesians* a Christian is one who has an appreciation of his spiritual blessings through union with Christ (1:3-14). He realises that it is by grace that God has made him alive in Christ (2:1-10). A professor of the Faith will, if he is genuine, show respect for the unity of the church and for her teachings (4:1-16). He will be concerned to live a life of practical holiness which includes the arena of the home — wives, husbands, children and parents (4:17 – 6:4). Concerning those who apply for baptism, discreet enquiry should be made as to their behaviour at home (5:22 – 6:4) and at work (6:5-9). This may not be possible, but no Christian testimony can be accepted as credible if the person in question lives inconsistently at home or at work. Certainly it is not perfection that is being advocated. But we are concerned about credibility. We must insist that the profession of faith must be credible before both Christians and non-Christians.

So far we have seen that the elements of doctrine, experience and practice must be present if faith is to be credible. We have seen that the emphasis on practical holy living is very strong and is stronger by far than that on feelings or emotions that can so often prove to be unreliable or temporary.

In the *first epistle of John* the apostle shows that the experimental factor is at the heart of Christianity. 'We love because he first loved us' (1 Jn. 4:19). Love for God is first. But it is easy to say, 'I love God.' How is that love proved? God has proved his love to us by action. He has given his Son. We prove our love to God by loving one another. It is not difficult to see why so much stress is laid on practice when we observe how deficient we are in love for others. John gives three tests for the testing of a Christian profession: the doctrinal, the social and the moral. A true Christian will believe correctly (4:2), he will live correctly (2:29) and he will regard his brothers rightly, that is with love (3:14). I have given only three references, but these tests recur in John's epistles over and over again.

This overview of our subject has been brief and selective. Many other tests or signs of a credible profession could be given, such as 'turning from idols to serve the living and true God' (1 Thess. 1:9) and learning to control the body (1 Thess. 4:4), but enough has been presented to substantiate the claim that recognition of what a Christian is is the business and coinage of the New Testament.

A right appreciation of the grace of God will always preserve us from wrong attitudes in making judgments. We must never be censorious or proud (Matt. 7:1-5), yet at the same time the Christian is commanded by Christ to exercise his powers of discernment (Matt. 7:6 and 15-20; 1 Cor. 2:15).

Reader, from these pages you have seen what a Christian is. Are you one? If not, why not? Why do you delay? What prevents you from coming now to Christ? Do you believe? Have you turned from sin? Perhaps you reply affirmatively, yes! Well, that is excellent! May I then ask you whether you have been baptised as a believer? No? Why not? What hinders you? You believe, you repent and yet have not been baptised? What does Peter say? 'Repent and be baptised every one of you.' Surely that includes you!

[1]*Baptism in the New Testament,* G. R. Beasley-Murray, p. 252.

The testimony of believer's baptism for our children

14

THE unity and diversity of the covenants is a subject large and profound. God's covenant was with his people whom he rescued out of Egypt. In the Old Testament it was necessary that there be a strong emphasis on the uniqueness of Israel as a nation. Every child was born with the privilege of covenant status. Within the nation into which they were born personal salvation was experienced by repentance and faith in the same way as in the New Testament. The difference was that their sacrifices represented the sacrifice to come. They believed on God's future provision for salvation: we believe in the accomplished reality.

The emphasis on a nation held together by birth and by blood-tie no longer exists. The Old Covenant has passed away completely (Heb. 8:13). With the coming of Christ the middle wall of partition has been broken down and now all believers, Jews and Gentiles, are one in Christ Jesus (Eph. 2:11-22). The body of Christ forms a new holy nation (1 Pet. 2:9). The children of believers no longer have their attention directed to the privileges of their physical birth. Rather they are taught that the way to the new birth is through hearing the Word (1 Pet. 1:22,23). The privileges of the Gospel are immeasurably superior to Old Testament privileges. The book of Hebrews fully demonstrates the superiority of the New Covenant over the Old. Christ is superior to Moses as a prophet and exceeds Aaron as priest. All the privileges of such a superior ministry are set before our children. Birth into a Christian family means birth into immense advantage and privilege. The privilege is the reality of Gospel nurture and teaching. The blessing lies not in the mark of an external sign but in the Gospel itself. The sign follows only when the reality has been appropriated. Our children are prayed for, protected and instructed in the home. There they see lived out day by day the life of the New Covenant. In addition they enjoy the prayers, teaching, preaching and nurture of the Christian church. Nowhere in the Bible are we told to encourage our children to trust in the fact of their birth privilege. On the contrary, personal faith and personal repentance are stressed. We are to take our children to Christ. We are always to set Christ before them in his all-sufficiency. We are to discourage all trust in self-merit. Moreover we are to stress that our faith and our parenthood cannot save them. Only Christ can save them. They are the victims of original sin in exactly the same way as are all other members of the human race. They are guilty of Adam's sin. They are destitute of that righteousness in which Adam was created. They were born at enmity to God with corrupt, unspiritual natures in an identical way to all others. They have by birth inherited natures which are wholly inclined to evil and opposite to all spiritual good. In no way have they escaped the awful implications of the fall. This we teach them to recognise.

The only difference between them and children of unbelieving households is that they are surrounded by those means designed to rescue them from their plight.

Commended to them at all times by their parents and by the church is salvation by faith in Christ. This commendation is supported and illustrated by the holy and beautiful life of faith that flows out of justification. As we have seen, believers' baptism portrays this salvation and portrays the saving work of Christ in his death and resurrection. The ordinance spells out that union that believers have with their Lord. That is what our children are to look forward to. That is what they are to seek. We do not direct their attention back into history to a birth privilege. We ourselves are living epistles of the truth. We constantly point our children to our Redeemer. Yet they are not to trust in any birth privilege for salvation, only Christ. As we have repented of sin and continue to make sin our enemy so they are directed to do likewise.

Compared with those who are born into unbelieving homes our children have these privileges of nurture, prayers and example as well as the glorious privilege of preaching which God declares is his instrument of power to save.

We are unjustly accused of being individualistic in contrast to being body-minded or corporate minded. The baptism of infants, we are told, ensures the unity of the body and puts the emphasis on the corporate nature of the household and church.

In response to that charge we declare that we are very jealous for the unity of Christian households and for the oneness of the Christian church. It is because we are concerned for the unity of our households that we lay such tremendous emphasis on repentance and faith, for without that there can never be unity.

However well intended infant baptism may be, it rebounds on those who practise it and is the enemy of unity. Infant baptism is based on presumption. It is presumed that the infant is elect or it is presumed that the infant is regenerate, or will become regenerate, and thereby have faith. All such presumption is disastrous. The children grow up unbelieving and that unbelief divides the Christian home. When they have been given church membership prematurely, but do not savingly believe, that unbelief divides the church.

It cannot be denied that the tendency is for children of believing households to grow up to be well-behaved, respectable, restrained, nominal believers. They see the good, they benefit from the immense wisdom and strength of Bible instruction, yet they show no signs of union with Christ. They are good listeners but have no prayer life. They possess no heart love for Christ. It is common in non-Baptist circles for such 'children of the covenant' to be included in church membership. All they have to do is attend catechism or confirmation classes, give correct answers and avoid anything offensive or scandalous.

But that is not the New Covenant procedure. The new covenant means that God's laws are written on the mind and heart. Faith which leads a person into union with Christ is essential. Faith we hold forth as crucial and essential. It can never be, and ought not to be presumed. Presumption is fatal to interests of souls and certainly fatal to the best interests of our children.

While we do everything in our power to maintain the spiritual unity of our families by directing our children into the way of salvation, we note our Lord's warning that his Gospel does divide. He did not come 'to bring peace, but a sword'. 'A man's enemies will be the members of his own household' (Matt. 10:34,36). Division comes when some believe and some do not. Division comes if some of the children do not embrace Christ. There is no absolute guarantee that all members of every family will believe. Faith is the only ground for the new covenant seal of baptism. Any departure from that is a violation of justification by faith alone. What has been said here accords well with Acts 2:39. The promise is indeed to our children. It is not a certainty but a promise. That promise is realised only in the call of God. Note that Peter goes on to declare that it is, 'for all whom the Lord our God will call'.

Likewise 1 Corinthians 7:14 accords fully with what has been said: 'For the unbelieving husband has been sanctified through his wife, and the unbelieving wife has been sanctified through her believing husband. Otherwise your children would be unclean, but as it is, they are holy.' The root meaning of holy, or sanctify, is, to be set apart. The word 'holy' is also used in the sense of definitive sanctification (1 Cor. 6:11), and progressive sanctification (1 Thess. 4:7). That the term is not being used in either of these ways, definitive or progressive, is clear in this case. Paul is specific about it: the partner *is unbelieving*. The partner is not sanctified by spiritual union with Christ (definitive sanctification) or by indwelling, progressive holiness. In what sense then is the unbelieving partner sanctified? What exactly is meant? It is the root meaning of the word 'holy', namely *set apart* that provides the answer. The unbelieving partner is set apart as far as privilege is concerned. The apartness is an apartness to privilege, a privilege which is not enjoyed where there is no believing partner. It is likewise with the children in homes of one believing parent. The advantage of having one believing parent gives them a distinction of privilege not afforded to those in unbelieving homes. But whether that privilege is to be effective has yet to be seen. That is precisely what Paul says when he declares, who knows whether the unbelieving partner may yet be saved? (1 Cor. 7:16). When that unbelieving partner does believe then baptism can follow. The same applies to the children.

At this point it will be helpful to observe that what is practised as infant baptism is something entirely different from New Testament baptism. The difference can be noted as follows:

Baptism of infants	Believers' baptism
1. Is imposed on the infants without their consent	Is voluntarily entered into
2. Is received unconsciously, the infant having no idea of what is happening	Is entered into with a full appreciation of the significance and meaning of the ordinance
3. Is received with complete passivity (although in some cases a strong vocal protest is made!)	Is entered into actively as the candidate steps down to be buried and entrusts himself to be raised up again
4. Is administered on the presumption that the infant will one day exercise repentance and faith	Is entered into on the New Testament practice and procedure of recognising a living, credible profession of repentance and faith
5. Is proceeded with on the basis of the faith of the parents, that is that one or both believe	Is proceeded with on the basis of the New Covenant, that is, the candidate knows the Lord; he has a living faith of his own
6. Is proceeded with on the basis of covenant status and descent, that is, physical birth	Is proceeded with on the basis of the new covenant of spiritual birth into the family of Christ
7. Confers upon the infant the presumption that he is a Christian so long as he is consistent	Confirms the fact that the candidate has now come from darkness to light, from Satan to God, from worldliness to holiness
8. Confers upon the infant the presumption of right to church membership	Symbolises the ingrafting of the new believer not only into Christ, but also into his body, the Church, of which he now becomes a member

9. Confers upon the infant the presumption of right to the Lord's Table	Introduces the believer to the Lord's Table for the first time, on the sole basis of the New Covenant, that is, he now knows the Lord
10. Introduces a syndrome of looking back to something which can never be recalled, or remembered, or felt, but only imagined	Establishes a conscious historical fact of entrance into Christ and his body, the Church, by faith, with all the new responsibilities now voluntarily undertaken, always to be remembered and referred to, as is the case with all the N.T. references

The contrast between the two practices should be obvious. The antithesis is apparent. Infant baptism is something entirely different from believers' baptism.

The baby boys of the Old Covenant had a physical mark put upon them. We are not required to do that. Our responsibility is to bring our children up in the training and instruction of the Lord (Eph. 6:4). That is a continual responsibility of about two decades' length of time.

Reference has already been made to the privileges of the means of grace conveyed by the light and example of the New Covenant which far outshine the privileges of the Old Covenant. As we have seen, our children are blessed with the innumerable advantages of a Christian home, godly parents, godly living, the fruit of the Spirit, Biblical instruction and prayers. The light, protection, counsel and loving care which unite in a believing household joined to a believing church constitute advantages and privileges which can never be equalled in any other place, family or environment.

A momentary sacramental act for an infant who can never recall the occasion is one thing. The constant, gracious influences of the Christian home and Christian church is another. The latter has Biblical warrant, the former has not.

John the Baptist counselled the Jews as follows: 'And do not begin to say to yourselves, "We have Abraham as our Father" ' (Luke 3:8). In other words, we are taught not to depend or rely upon anything intrinsic in birth, or national status, or credit by way of parentage. To what then must we look? The answer is that we must rely completely on sovereign grace. In the Bible grace stands for the favour of salvation which proceeds from the love of God alone, without any consideration of human merit in any shape or form. The very essence of grace is that it comes to the undeserving. By sovereign is meant that God is free to bestow grace as he wills. He is not bound to save his enemies. He says, 'I will have mercy on whom I will have mercy' (Rom. 9:15).

Of course, it is not easy to look to sovereign grace alone. By nature we desire to find some merit of our own, or see some merit in our children, because they are so close to us and spring from us.

Why, it may be asked, should we be shut up to sovereign grace, and not find reason for the salvation of our children in their privileged position by birth? The answer should be clear. It is that when God does bring about the conversion of our children, all the glory for that is attributed to him. All is to the praise of his glorious grace.

What advantage do our children have then over those who are born into unbelieving homes? Already we have seen the advantage to be superabundant. Salvation is near to our children. It is right by them. In the case of those born into non-Christian homes the prospect is terrifying because everything militates against their coming to understand, trust in Christ, and believe in the Scriptures. Ignorance prevails. Indeed, it is worse than ignorance, because in most modern homes prejudice against the Bible prevails.

Christian parents can be encouraged to think upon the fact that the Lord who plans from eternity and orders all things well, has already caused our children to be born into the circle where grace is mediated. Included in the means of grace are the prayers of God's people. How marvellous is the privilege of being surrounded by loving prayers throughout one's upbringing! And who can estimate the advantage of knowing the Scriptures from childhood? As Paul reminded Timothy, 'how from infancy you have known the holy Scriptures, which are able to make you wise for salvation through faith in Christ Jesus' (2 Tim. 3:15).

In addition to all the advantages outlined so far, the children of believing households are witnesses of the actual testimony of believers' baptism. Our children are not excluded from hearing the testimony of new converts, sometimes those of their own age. They observe the transformation of life in such new believers.

Then all that is involved in conversion is portrayed in the actual ordinance. The involvement of the new believers in baptism and the joy of the local church are witnessed. The entrance of converts into the enrichments and pleasures of the New Covenant, joyful union with Father, Son and Holy Spirit, are likewise observed. The Holy Spirit sometimes uses the ordinance of believers' baptism, together with the witness wrapped up therein to convince the unconverted ones of the reality of faith, and of their own need to come to Christ in trustful obedience.

What constitutes a valid baptism?

15

T HIS chapter deals with the practical problem of how to view the widespread practice of child baptism, and suggests principles by which we may discern whether the baptism of adults has been in accordance with Scripture.

The invalidity of Roman Catholic infant baptism
The testimony or witness of baptism is destroyed when the ordinance is administered to those who do not qualify by Scripture. It is sometimes supposed that the Mass is Rome's greatest error, with the claim of the transubstantiation of the elements. But in baptism the claim is made that the momentous act of new birth takes place – an act infinitely greater in power than the changing of bread into flesh. The visit of Pope John Paul to Britain during May 1982 confirmed that the assumption of baptismal regeneration is one foundation on which the Roman Catholic system is built.[1]

Before examining the baptism service let us remind ourselves of the biblical definition of regeneration. We note firstly that it is an act of God. Ephesians 1:19, 20 tells us that the power exerted by God in the new birth of a single soul is comparable with the power employed in raising Christ from the dead. God alone can make a dead sinner to be spiritually alive in Christ; it is a creative work exceeding the wonderful creativity exerted in the formation of the material universe. Moreover regeneration is a creative and powerful act of God which cannot be undone.

Secondly regeneration consists of a fundamental change in the very nature of a person. Before, the person was an enemy of God, and paralysed as far as spiritual activity was concerned (Rom. 8:7, 8). When God acts to regenerate, that person is given a 'new heart' (Ez. 11:19) and is a 'new creation' (2 Cor. 5:17). There is a transformation of the outlook. The affections and mind are changed by a creative act of God. The scriptures everywhere insist that regeneration is from above, that it comes by the will of God, and that the Holy Spirit is like the wind — totally beyond the manipulative power of man. We can be sure that in this matter God is not controlled by ministers, priests, bishops or popes! (John 1:12, 13; 3:1-18).

We are now in a position to compare the Roman Catholic performance of baptism with this exalted biblical doctrine of the new birth. In this service there is an invocation calling on Mary, Joseph, and the other saints to pray.[2] Then: 'The prayer of Exorcism and the Anointing with Oil of Catechumins prepare the child for the coming of the new life of God in baptism! At the font the priest says 'My dear brethren, God uses the sacrament of water to give his divine life to those who believe in him. Let us turn to him and ask him to pour his gift of life from this font on this child he has chosen.' The waters are blessed, the parents and God-parents profess faith, water is poured three times over the child's head. The child is anointed with Chrism, with the following prayer: 'God the Father of our Lord Jesus Christ has freed you from sin, given you a new birth by water and the Holy Spirit, and welcomed you into his holy people. . . .' Then the child is clothed in a white garment, with the prayer '. . . you have become a new creation, and have clothed yourself in Christ . . .' A parent lights a candle and the priest says 'This child of yours has been enlightened by Christ. He is always to walk as a child of the light. . . .' At the conclusion of the rite the priest says 'My dear brethren, this child has been reborn in baptism. He is now called the child of God. There follows the Lord's Prayer and the blessing.

The above claims are astonishing; in some nations over ninety per cent of the population are supposed by infant baptism to be regenerated, united with Christ! The number includes multitudes of spiritually dead people who possess none of the marks of New Testament believers. Yet all who have been baptised have 'a right to take part in the Eucharist'. This is dealt with more fully in the chapter 'Various views of nonbaptists considered'.

It is important to note that it is a sign of apostate religion when men claim to possess the power to control that which belongs to God alone. Over the years the Roman Catholic Church has increasingly taken to herself claims of controlling salvation, the claim of baptismal regeneration being the most blatant, followed by the claim in the Mass to resacrifice Christ over and over again.

The invalidity of Anglican infant baptism
The Anglican service allows for infants to be dipped or for water to be poured, the Trinitarian formula for baptism being used. The 'priest' in prayer says of those he has thus baptised: 'Lord God our Father, maker of heaven and earth, we thank you that by your Holy Spirit these children have been born again into new life, adopted for your own, and received into the fellowship of your Church.'[3] These words are plain and the error of baptismal regeneration cannot be explained away.

The invalidity of all infant baptism
We have examined in detail the Roman Catholic administration of baptism and referred to the Anglican form, but what of a believer who was baptized as an infant in a Protestant church where baptismal regeneration is repudiated? How is he to regard his baptism? Even where the error of baptismal regeneration is not succumbed to, we have to conclude that *the testimony of baptism is non-existent unless the one who is being baptized has a valid confession of faith.* The absolute need for a credible profession of faith is examined presently. Suffice it here to say that the testimony provided for the world by infant baptism, whether administered by Protestant or Catholic, is negative and harmful. It is tragic to know that in this country as in many others the vast majority of people have been sprinkled as babies, and yet show no signs of spiritual life. The credibility of Christianity is destroyed for those such as Hindus or Muslims who do not understand the difference between nominal Christians and evangelical Bible-believing Christians.

The invalidity of Child baptism
Infant baptism is conducted upon the erroneous principle of presumption — presuming that God will perform the work of regeneration within all who are sprinkled. Presumption and the implicit claim of controlling the will and power of God, is increasingly to be found in evangelical churches today, where human decision is equalled with the divine act of regeneration. It is the custom to make 'Altar calls' at the end of services when people are invited to come forward and make a decision for Christ. The idea is that man possesses a power of will which he can exercise in such a way as to cause the new birth. Martin Luther described this error of free will as the root error of Rome. It is now the root error of professing evangelicalism. The will of man, rather than the priest sprinkling water, is supposed to instantly bring about regeneration. In some churches baptism soon follows the decision without adequate time to see whether there is genuine repentance and faith. It is very common to find large numbers of children and young people making such decisions and being baptized. God in his sovereignty *does* sometimes regenerate young children. They may sustain a credible profession and then may properly be baptised. But it is all too easy to persuade children, particularly the sensitive children of Christian parents, to make a decision and be baptized. There are reliable ministers within large denominations in America such as the Southern Baptist Convention who assert that the majority of those who have been baptized on the basis of a decision made when young, do not evidence the marks, of regeneration. Thus we have masses of people who are nominal Baptists just as there are nominal Roman Catholics or nominal Anglicans.

What constitutes a valid baptism?
These practices, Roman Catholic and Protestant, raise the vital question — what is a valid baptism? The answer can be sought by considering the following factors, 1. A valid confession, 2. A valid mode, 3. A valid minister,

4. A valid church. Do all these have to be right for a baptism to be right? The last two issues are straightforward and can be dealt with briefly. Concerning a valid minister we may suppose that Judas Iscariot possessed eminent gifts, otherwise the disciples would not have been surprised when he was exposed as a traitor. Say you were baptized by a minister who later departs himself from the faith? Does that render your baptism null and void? Certainly not! The whole transaction was conducted sincerely and according to the truth. That the minister or pastor who officiated has failed himself does not invalidate your baptism.

In considering the question of a valid church it is necessary to say that the baptisms in cults like Jehovah's Witnesses and Mormons are totally unacceptable. If the apostle Paul rebaptized the twelve Ephesians (Acts 19:1-7) because of the inadequacies of John's baptism, especially with regard to the Trinity, how much more do we reject baptisms which have taken place within the context of religion which is hostile to the Gospel.

For a church to be true it needs to bear the character of a New Testament church or assembly. The main marks are usually described as, 1. The faithful preaching of the Word, 2. The faithful administration of church discipline, 3. The maintenance of baptism and the Lord's supper, 4. Evidence of spiritual life by way of godliness evidenced in the members of the church.

Suppose for instance that a church degenerates through losing the first mark. Suppose that a liberal minister who denies the central truths of the Bible is called to lead. I recall travelling in America during 1982 and coming across a case of a once exceedingly prosperous church with a membership of about 1,000. It was however in the throes of falling apart. A liberal minister had been installed. Most of the faithful had left as a result and only a remnant remained. Now say a young believer ignorant of these issues gets baptized into such a church? Does that invalidate his baptism? Surely not! He has proceeded with a biblical well-grounded faith and sincerity. In due course he will surely be guided to a better and safer assembly where he will be nurtured. The defective nature of the church does not invalidate his baptism.

We consider next the mode of baptism in the case of sincere believers who, being misguided or ignorant of the symbolism required in baptism, have been sprinkled but not buried or immersed. Is their baptism valid? My answer is no! The foremost meaning of union with Christ in his death, burial and resurrection has not been demonstrated. The other meaning likewise is absent, namely, the symbolism of sin being washed away (Acts 22:16). A parallel would be like going up to the Lord's Table and looking at the elements without partaking either of the bread or the wine. If a believer comes forward for baptism on the grounds of repentance and faith, his reasons have been sound. The pathway so far is correct but the mode is virtually non-existent. The Trinitarian formula may be used but no symbolism has been enacted. Therefore the believer should be properly baptized and together with the church into which he is being baptized rejoice in full biblical symbolism of his union with the Trinity.

What if a person does not have the physical health to be immersed? The answer is to simply accept the situation. Some bed-ridden saints are never able to attend the Lord's house or to be present at the Lord's Table. The ordinances in themselves do not save. The ordinances confirm and help us in our salvation. Where genuine physical handicaps prevent participation in the ordinances, the Holy Spirit is well able to make up the deficiency.

What about conditions in which there is definitely no prospect of an immersion? Take the Bushmen of the Kalahari. When we read the descriptions by eye-witness explorers like Laurens van der Post it is surprising to find that even Bushmen locate substantial pools of water. Nevertheless let us imagine them in the vastness of their trackless oceans of sand. The Bushmen are masters of simulation and could easily simulate a burial and resurrection in the sand which together with the pouring of some water could stand for the washing away of sin. The central meaning is what is to be aimed at. We have to avoid legalism on the one hand. On the other we must reject unnecessary neglect of commands which are plain.

The most complex question of all is a valid testimony. What makes or constitutes a credible profession of faith and repentance? This I have discussed elsewhere and described as the business and coinage of the New Testament. If a person is absolutely certain that he was immersed as a believer with a totally inadequate basis, and is quite sure that it was misguided and false, then if this is the case, the elders and experienced members of the church should be consulted.

If there is agreement that the baptism was premature and wholly without the first and essential basis of a credible testimony, then procedure on proper grounds should be followed. If there is doubt and the matter hinges on a question on doubt merely, or lack of assurance, then rebaptism is out of the question. It should be discouraged on the grounds that baptism is a once and for all ordinance. There is one baptism into Christ, just as there is only one new birth, one creation in Christ. That momentous event is the heart of the matter. The event is being portrayed. It is to be portrayed once only, and that on proper grounds. To sum up then: a valid baptism must be based on a credible testimony of repentance and faith, it must be what it is in itself, that is immersion or burial.

---

[1] The confirmation of this fact was illustrated vividly in the gathering of huge concourses of people all of whom are regarded as Christian on the basis of infant baptism. Discussion with individuals soon reveals the extent to which these adherents to the Roman Catholic system are

nominal and destitute of any idea of what constitutes a saving knowledge of Christ.
[2] All quotations from *'The New Baptism Book'* April 1981, pp. 12-17.
[3] *The Alternative Service Book,* 1980, p. 248.

Illustrations

Pastor F. Buhler of 9 Rue des Charpentiers, 68100, Mulhouse, France, has built up a folio of information on baptistries of early centuries uncovered by archaeologists in recent years. Five of these, one each for Spain, Greece, Corsica, Yugoslavia and France have been depicted by way of illustration.

The construction and size of these baptistries point to the mode of immersion. As the centuries passed it would appear that the size of baptistries diminished. For example one baptistry (not included in the illustrations) unearthed at Lyons, France, shows a three-stage reduction in size from 3.00m. width to 2.34m. and finally to 1.97m. The reason can only be surmized. The author baptizes in a pool with a width less than 1.97m. and finds it wholly adequate. Further information will doubtless emerge as archaeological research goes on in the future.

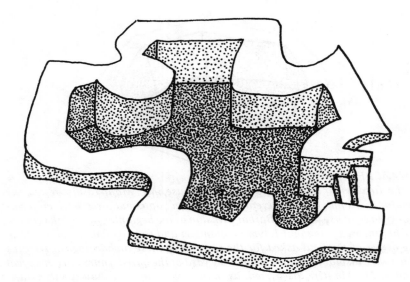

1. PHILIPPI, Macedonia (Greece)
The excavations (1958-1974) of a paleochristian church called Church D or
Oktogon at Philippi led to the discovery of a cross-shaped baptistry decorated
with marble plates — of approximately 9 x 10m., in which were found the
remains of a Maltese cross-shaped font which must have been 1.20m. deep
originally and over 2m. between opposite walls. Three steps existed in each
branch of the cross. The present depth is 0.80m. The interior of the font was
decorated with marble plates as well. The Oktogon is known as early as the 4th
century and the baptistry may be dated from the 4th or 5th century. It was no
doubt built for immersion of adults.

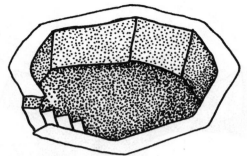

2. CAZERES (Haute-Garonne)

In the fields near Cazeres, South of Toulouse, Mr. Maniére discovered the remains of a small church, several tombs and a baptismal piscina which seems to have been in use until the Barbar invasion at the beginning of the 5th century. The piscine was octagonal 1.39m. in diameter and from 0.40m. to 0.48m. deep. The owner of the field asked for the removal of these archaeological remains which were displaced to the set up in the yard of the parish church. To his great surprise Mr. Maniére discovered, as he removed the font, that exactly underneath was a piscina of the same shape but 1.13m. deep. This font was probably of the second half of the 4th century and served for the immersion of adults. This discovery is of great significance as to the mode of baptism prior to the 5th century.

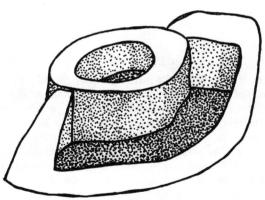

3. SRIMA near Sibenick, YUGOSLAVIA

In a relatively important complex of a double basilica with adjoining baptistry of 6.10m. x 4.55m. a circular font of 0.75m. in diameter and 0.67m. in depth was discovered the top of which was 0.26m. above the floor level. Underneath a cross-shaped piscina was found about 1.60m. long from one branch of the cross to the other one way and about 1.23m the other way. The depth was 0.77m. If the circular font was large enough for the immersion of children, the lower font permitted the immersion of adults quite easily.

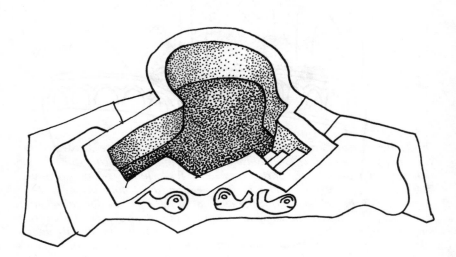

4. *MARIANA near Bastia, CORSICA*
A baptistry (6.50m. x 6.50m.) with walls preserved at a height of 1.20m. has been discovered. Some of the original mosaics with which the baptistry was decorated are preserved. These include fish, ducks, dolphins, deer and the four rivers of paradise. The impression is one of copious water supplies. Only the fish are attempted in drawing shown.

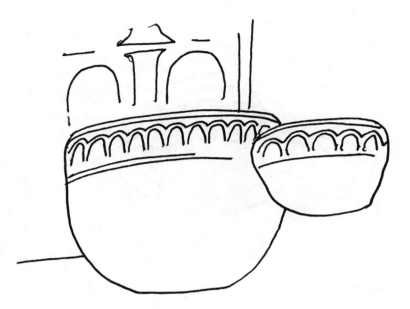

5. CASTELLO di AMPURIAS Prov. of Gerona, SPAIN

A very peculiar font can be seen in the church of Castello. Some think that the larger font could have been used for adults, whereas the other smaller font on the side of the larger is being used for infant baptism. The size of the larger font is 1.20m. interior diameter, depth 0.81m. The smaller is 0.85m. exterior diameter and 0.64m. high. It was locked so we could not measure the interior. We presume it must be about 0.40m. deep and 0.50m. wide which would allow infant immersion.

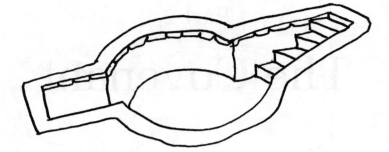

6. EPHESUS

Excavated at Ephesus is a baptistry a coloured photograph of which appears in the Lion handbook, 'The History of Christianity' p. 173. Details of size and age are not provided. The copious nature of the structure bears testimony to the mode of baptism employed.

Part 2

The Covenant

Unity, the covenant and baptism

HOW much do Reformed Baptists have in common with Reformed Paedobaptists (herein after called Reformed non-Baptists)? To answer that we have to go back to the age when Protestant Christianity was confessed in credal form.

It is with considerable justification that the Westminster Confession of Faith is regarded widely as the finest statement of belief to have come from the Reformation Period. It was a product of the Puritans and it came at the apex of the Puritan period. The Puritan divines convened from 1643 to 1649. What they formulated has formed the doctrinal foundation of Presbyterianism.

Baptists in England acknowledged the merit of the Westminster Confession. In 1677 they formulated their own Confession based upon the Westminster Confession. Identical to it in most statements, it differs from it in some parts and particularly in the chapters dealing with baptism, the nature of the church and church government.[1]

Persecution of dissenters was fierce in those days and it was not until 1689 that the Baptists were able to publish their Confession which they called the London Baptist Confession of Faith. It is a document which has been used by Baptists of Reformed conviction ever since. For instance C. H. Spurgeon in 1856, during the second year of his ministry in London, had the 1689 Confession republished and avowed it to be the statement which accorded with his own beliefs. In 1976 Carey Publications, which is connected with the Cuckfield Baptist Church in Sussex, had the Confession transposed into modern English and gave it the title *A Faith to Confess*. By 1979 three editions had been published. Churches all over the world have adopted it as their Confession.

Now we should remember that there are 32 chapters in the Confession.

Of those our Reformed non-Baptist brethren would accord in every detail with 29 chapters.   Moreover this accord or unity in believing would include the grand centralities of the Christian Faith, the authority of the bible, justification by faith, assurance, sanctification, and so on.

As we view the history of the church we see that God has his own way of bringing truth to life.   Very often he allows error or heresy to spread and then to his own glory raises up defenders of the faith, often powerful preachers who proclaim the truth with such clarity that it defeats the heresies that have spread.   Martin Luther is the most obvious example. Justification by faith alone and by grace alone was a marvellous biblical truth in contrast to the miserable catalogue of works by which people were urged to try and earn their salvation.

In our times basic truths either have been forgotten or are being challenged. The sovereignty of God is one such basic truth which has been either forgotten or distorted in Baptist churches all over the world.   Therefore the rediscovery and expositions of the doctrines of God's sovereign grace in salvation can cause tremendous upheavals in churches where the preaching has been of a non-expository or shallow kind.

But there are other challenges today.   There is the challenge of Modernism and neo-orthodoxy which rejects the view that the Scriptures are without error.   There is also the challenge of Ecumenism especially in view of the willingness of many to unite with the Church of Rome now mightily invigorated under the leadership of a versatile and energetic new Pope, John Paul II, the first non-Italian for over 450 years.   The greater the man the greater become the errors to which he gives his emphatic endorsement.

We do well then to review those truths which unite us.   In considering the question of where to begin we could start with Scripture.   It should be obvious that if we do not have unity there then we have no unity at all, because the Scriptures provide the foundations for all matters of faith and practice.

Or should we begin with experience?   We tend to take the doctrine of the inspiration of Scripture for granted and are not easily moved in our emotions and feelings about that truth.   In contrast, however, we are very soon moved in our emotions and feelings by considering the implications of the sovereignty of God especially as it affects salvation.   Many of us have found that truth to be overwhelming.   It is something that has revolutionised our minds and lives.   A discovery of the implications of the sovereignty of God has transformed thousands and shaken many churches.   Therefore, while respecting all truth and the place of logic and order, I intend to enlarge most on those matters which in our days are proving powerful and which serve to awaken and rouse us where we need to be stirred.   We will begin therefore with the Reformation, then consider the subject of Scripture, and thereafter devote most attention to the implications of God's sovereignty.

The factors which unite Reformed Baptists and Reformed non-Baptists are as follows:

1. *A shared thankfulness for the Reformation*

'The Reformation from Popery in the sixteenth century was the greatest event, or series of events, that has occurred since the close of the Canon of Scripture; and the men who are really entitled to be called the "Leaders of the Reformation" have a claim to more respect and gratitude than any other body of uninspired men that have ever influenced or adorned the church.' So wrote William Cunningham.[2] When we think of the religious ignorance, gross superstitition and spiritual darkness that prevailed in Europe before the Reformation we must truly marvel at the great change that was brought about in recovering the Gospel light which for so long had been extinguished. The Reformation of the sixteenth century reclaimed the Bible for the common people and restored preaching to the foremost place designed for it by God. Christian truth was clarified in a number of excellent confessions of faith. Biblical doctrines which had been all but buried since the time of Augustine were re-established. The bondage of the human will, the total corruption of human nature through original sin, the sovereign election of God the Father according to his own will and not through works or faith foreseen, justification by faith alone, the sanctification of God's elect by the Holy Spirit—these are just some of the main truths made clear through the Reformation.

2. *A common belief in the infallible Word of God as the only authority for faith and practice*

To clarify this point we need to go back to the doctrinal decrees and ecclesiastical canons of the Councils of Nicaea (325), Constantinople (381), Ephesus (431), and Chalcedon (451). The first two of these councils dealt in particular with the doctrine of the Trinity, the third with the doctrine of the Person of Christ.[3] The life of the Church does not depend upon Councils, but with interest we observe that these early Councils based their findings on Scripture alone and were used to clarify teachings which had been obscure.

This matter is relevant today because in the Second Vatican Council the authority of Roman Catholic Church tradition was powerfully reasserted.[4] For Rome tradition has an equal authority with Scripture. In this way the unique authority of Scripture is denied and the Word of God made powerless and void.

As Reformed believers we have the essential foundation of trust in the inerrancy of Scripture in common. For us the Scriptures are infallible and form the only authority for all belief and teaching. Modern scholarship rejects the claim of inerrancy of Scripture. Neo-orthodoxy, while posing as a friend of Scripture, destroys the Bible by rejecting the historical time-space events such as the literal resurrection of Christ. Today evangelical denominations which are non-Reformed are tending more and more to compromise with what is known as the New Evangelicalism which rejects the infallibility of the Bible. Reformed Christians, therefore, have a vital contribution to make in defending and preserving the Gospel in an age when the Bible is being attacked in an unprecedented way, not only by the unbelieving world, but by those who pose as Christians within the churches. Moreover, many of the seminaries which are so crucial for the thorough training and preparation of candidates for the ministry are now controlled by those who deny the faith and reject the authority of Scripture. Princeton Seminary in the U.S.A. and the Free University of Amsterdam are examples of this tragic situation.

3. *The sovereignty of God and predestination*

One of the foremost characteristics of the Reformed Faith is belief in the Sovereignty of God. The Almighty One is sovereign in creation.

> *By the word of the Lord were the heavens made,*
> *Their starry host by the breath of his mouth* (Ps. 33:6).[5]

There seemed to be no struggle on God's part to create the universe nor did it take him long to do it. Immediately he commanded it, it was done. So will it be in the resurrection. In a moment, in the twinkling of an eye we shall be changed.

This view of God's sovereign, omnipotent power is the reason why it is rare to find those of Reformed persuasion compromising on the subject of creation.

We believe too that God is sovereign in the history of this world. From all eternity he decreed all that should come to pass in time. All the governments and all the rulers of this world are under the sovereign rule of God. All the fallen angels, Lucifer and his hosts of demons, are under God's control and cannot do anything without his permission (Job 1:12). The archangels and angels of heaven are likewise under his sovereign administration.

> *He does as he pleases with the powers of heaven and the peoples of the earth,*
> *No-one can hold back his hand or say to him: What have you done?*
> (Dan. 4:35)

These views of God's sovereign omnipotence exalt God and help us to see him as he really is, high, majestic, lifted up. A right perception of the majestic Godhood of God humbles us to proper dimensions. We are brought down to see ourselves as we truly are, unworthy creatures of the dust. Only when we are so humbled are we able to render acceptable worship. A right view of the supremacy of God fills us with respect, awe and thankfulness. We draw unspeakable comfort in knowing that we belong to one who has sovereign control over all things.

A strong faith and sweet sense of security is afforded to those who know God as their sovereign Father. The faith strengthens the believer in times of sorrow and loss because our sovereign God has promised and is able to cause his kingdom to triumph over all evil.

Surely we have far more unity with a humble God-fearing non-Baptist who with us has a profound respect for these attributes of God than with a proud Baptist who argues against the sovereignty of God? This leads us to the heart of this matter.

4. *The sovereign grace of God in salvation*

What is the very essence of the Reformed awakening that has been taking place over the last twenty years? Answer: A personal, inward, spiritual realisation by Christians of the fact that they are redeemed by the sovereign grace of God alone apart from any other factor. In my book *The Believer's Experience* I refer to the free-grace experience as the deepest spiritual experience in the Christian's life. What is the free-grace experience? It is an experimental realisation that we are saved through God's election and not through anything we have done. It is not that God foresaw that we would exercise faith and on that basis he chose us, rather he saw that we were hopelessly lost and that we would always hate and reject him. When we were still powerless, Christ died for the ungodly (Rom. 5:6). Note the words 'powerless and ungodly'. The action that rescues us from a life of ungodliness and from spiritual deadness is an action of sovereign grace.

The Bible teaches total depravity and original sin, truths which many modern evangelical churches have taken for granted, but the implications of which they do not understand. This matter is one of the utmost importance and should be constantly taught because without these truths there can never be a proper appreciation of the free grace of God.

We will examine the implications of original sin presently and see that all children are the same whether born of Christian parents or not. But first let us deal with what we call total depravity.

Total depravity does not mean that man is as bad as he possibily can be. By the gift of God's common grace many non-Christians show much virtue and goodness. Total depravity means that man is depraved toward God in the whole of his being including his heart and will. He does not love God. Therefore he will not come to God. That is the crux of the matter. Of himself fallen man will never, never come. He has to be made willing by the work of the Holy Spirit to come. Indeed a mighty work of new birth or new spiritual creation must take place if he is to come to Christ.

Free grace means that God *freely* without any constraint outside of himself bestows his salvation on whomsoever he pleases. He is not obligated to save any enemy or rebel. If he saves anyone it is because of grace and that grace is free from obligation (Rom. 3:24).

The great majority of what we call evangelical (Bible-believing) Christians today still believe in what we call free will. To them it is man that chooses. Hence (although they do not like it to be said) it is really man who saves himself. Or shall we say man gives God that little bit of essential help that is needed. That is what makes the difference between the saved and unsaved. This reasoning prevails in spite of plain statements such as 'There is no-one who seeks God' (Rom. 3:11).

Let me illustrate the practical importance of this point. Like all churches, we have people who attend services and then disappear. Such visitors have declared that they have benefited from the preaching and have appreciated the fellowship of the church. Nevertheless they do not return. We learn afterwards that the real reason why they decided not to join with us is that they believe in free will. They simply could not accept this Reformed teaching about salvation. Most Baptists admire Spurgeon so we are quick to point out that he preached the bondage of the will. But this makes little difference because it is easy to ignore those sermons by Spurgeon in which he is so eloquent on these matters. Naturally our best argument is from Scripture but in the final analysis it is the prerogative of the Holy Spirit to reveal these truths. Lest my readers gain a false impression from all this let me assure them most heartily that I believe in a balanced presentation of doctrine. I try to avoid overstatement. Like most preachers in our circles I preach through the Bible systematically, book by book. Whatever is in the text I attempt faithfully to declare. If it is John 10 or Hebrews 10 then I preach on particular redemption in the form and proportion that is found in those passages. There are many evangelical preachers, however, who are like grasshoppers. When they come to a subject like election they simply jump over it. Yet that is not a truth easily avoided. This is not something confined to Ephesians and Romans. In 1 Peter you will find it in the first verse and in 1 Thessalonians you will find it by the fourth verse! You cannot move through the first chapter of 1 Corinthians without coming face to face with the truth that were it not for God's sovereign action in election nobody would be saved.

Now let us examine the question of original sin which is the source of total depravity. This doctrine means that all the children of Adam are born with corrupt natures whereby they are utterly indisposed, disabled and made opposite to all that is spiritually good, and rendered wholly inclined by disposition to that which is contrary to the mind and will of God—and that continually. In order of importance these realities about man together with the holy character of the eternal God and his moral law precede other truths.   Unless a sense of guilt and lostness is imbibed there will never be a desire for salvation.   These are basic matters.   They are matters we have in common with many Reformed non-Baptists— matters which unhappily are not always shared with Baptists.

It perplexes us that some Reformed non-Baptists deny this teaching of original sin in practice.   They presume that their children are Christians. Dr. A. Kuyper, Sr., and Prof. John Murray are among the main proponents of this very serious error.[5]   Certainly our children are not pagans in the sense that they are untutored by Christian upbringing, but parentage does not remove original sin.   Upbringing does not cancel original sin. Baptism whether of infants or adults does not obliterate original sin.   Let it be asserted as clearly as language permits—*all children of believers without exception are born in original sin* (Ps. 51:5).   Everyone of them is lost until he or she is saved by the Gospel of Jesus Christ.   Parents, you are urged not to lull your children into a false sense of security.   In hell they will curse you for it.   From the very beginning we must impress upon our children the necessity of their conversion.   They must be born again. They must believe unto salvation for themselves.   They must themselves be savingly joined to Christ.

I am sometimes amazed to find that children of Reformed non-Baptists, who show no evidence of salvation, no union with Christ and no spiritual life, have never ever been challenged by their parents or minister.   On a number of occasions the children of Dutch Reformed parents have come among us.   They presumed all was well until personally challenged by the necessity of conversion and the necessity of the new birth (see John ch. 3).   This has sometimes been the means used by God to bring them into personal union with Christ and for the first time to a living, saving, personal faith.

Because we believe in inter-church unity we do not teach those who are converted in this way to go back and be in conflict with their churches. But if they decide to live here then we insist that they submit with all the other converts to proper believers' Baptism and church membership. We cannot have double standards of one rule for some and a disobedience of Christ's commands for others.   Of course not all non-Baptists presume their children to be regenerate.

Deep concern to avoid the fatal presumption that our children are regenerate because of Christian upbringing is shared by Baptist and non-Baptists.   William Cunningham, a Reformed non-Baptist, wrote powerfully as follows:

> We believe that the notion of sacramental justification and regeneration, more or less distinctly developed, has always been, and still is, one of the most successful delusions which Satan employs for ruining men's souls, and that there is nothing of greater practical importance than to root out this notion from men's minds, and to guard them against its ruinous influence.   This can be done only by

impressing on them right views of the sacramental principle, or the general doctrine of the sacraments, and applying it fully both to baptism and the Lord's Supper; and especially by bringing out the great truths, that the sacraments are intended for believers, that they can be lawfully and beneficially received only when faith has been already produced, that they imply or suppose the previous existence of the great fundamental blessings of remission and regeneration; while, at the same time, they do not, simply as external acts or providential results, afford any proof or evidence of the possession of these blessings, or the existence of the faith with which it is invariably connected. These views go to the root of the matter, and if fully and faithfully applied, would prevent the fearful mischief, which cannot, we fear, be reached in any other way.[6]

(*British and Foreign Evangelical Review*, 1860, p. 939)

5. *A joint desire for true Christian worship*

For us the Bible is authoritative for everything, salvation, home and family life, church government and worship. We are not left to our own inventions when it comes to public worship. In the Roman Church the people watch a mysterious and symbolical performance called the Mass, something which is not prescribed by Scripture and which by its very nature is opposed to the finished work of Christ.

Our primary concern when we think about public worship is the presence and power of the Holy Spirit. What is it that will please him? That should be our obsession. Yet all too often we concentrate only on impressing men.

We do not gather to celebrate superstitious rituals. Nor do we gather to be entertained by performers, which is the case in some churches. We gather to hear the public reading of Scripture, to sing psalms and hymns in praise to God, to be led in prayer and to hear the preaching of the Word by those called, equipped, recognised by the church, and set apart for the awesome task of public ministry. In some churches today there is a trend towards the idea that no special qualifications are required to lead public worship. There is also opposition to the idea of the professional minister. The arguments sound plausible enough but in practice the result is one in which the standard of worship soon degenerates. Services become disjointed and poor in content. Worship is not for the uplifting of personalities or to focus attention on each other but for the exaltation of God.

There is truly a place for sharing and for Christian fellowship a practice which is often a strength and advantage in Baptist churches. Let us enjoy such Christian communion yet at the same time be sure that this is never gained at the expense of God-centred worship.

Worship should be joyful and full of thanksgiving. The whole person should be moved by the truth of Scripture to wonder, love and praise. Artificial means such as joking, lightness or frivolity are alien to true worship. A common desire to preserve high standards of preaching, public ministry and worship is an important factor common to Reformed Baptists and Reformed non-Baptists.

6. *The recovery of powerful, evangelical preaching*

We believe that the recovery of preaching which is Biblical and full of the Holy Spirit is the urgent need of our age. Preaching should be faithful to the whole counsel of God's Word. It should be doctrinal in the definitive sense of being faithful to biblical truth and crystal clear. It should be expository. The meaning of the text should be explained and applied. The lives of the preachers and of the hearers must feel and experience the power and application of the Gospel in all areas.

Preaching must be evangelical. It must be prophetic in the sense that the message comes from God. We believe that those who do not repent will be lost forever in a never-ending place of torment. Preaching therefore should be modelled on that of the apostles for boldness, urgency, integrity and power.

Every significant advance in the history of the church has come by a restoration of preaching. Martin Luther was a preacher of great stature. John Calvin preached daily. The Puritan age was an age of great preachers. After a miserable period in which philosophy dominated in the pulpits the great Awakening of the eighteenth century broke forth in a mighty conquering fashion through the agency of preachers like Whitefield and Wesley, men endued with power from on high to preach to multitudes.

We are not interested in preaching which is only intellectual, however correct it might be. We are concerned to see a resurrection of preaching which stirs the hearts and lives of the people. Nothing more or less will turn the rising tide of iniquity and evil in the world today.

Preaching of this kind will not be produced without hard work. Even though the age of the Holy Spirit had come in great power the apostles found it essential to devote themselves 'to prayer and the ministry of the word' (Acts 6:4). That delusion is fatal which leads some to think that because they have the spirit they can dispense with the tremendously exacting and often exhausting labour required for expository preaching. We must have the Holy Spirit in preparation and in delivery of sermonic materials. Indeed it is only by his enabling that we can survive in a calling which Paul described as so demanding that nobody is really equal to it (2 Cor. 2:14-17).

7. *A shared belief in the importance of biblical theology and the covenant*

The subject of biblical theology is one of foremost importance. Biblical theology is a study of history of divine revelation recorded in Scripture. Chester K. Lehman defines biblical theology as 'that branch of biblical interpretation which deals with the revelation of God to men in the light of the revealing activity of God, the spiritual experiences of men to whom he spoke, and the character of the written word'. He quotes Hermann Schultz's definition: 'Biblical Theology is that branch of the theological science which gives a historical presentation of revealed religion during the period of its growth.'[8]

Geerhardus Vos defines the subject as 'the process of the self revelation of God deposited in the Bible'.[9] Dr. Gustav Friedrich Oehler in his mighty treatise on this subject says, 'Biblical theology has the task of exhibiting the religion of the Bible according to its *progressive development* and *the variety of the forms in which it appears,*' and we have to follow 'the *gradual* progress by which the Old Testament revelation advanced to the completion of salvation in Christ.'[10] Observe Oehler's emphasis: *progressive, gradual, variety of forms.*

To develop this theme further we could say that God has at different times and ways entered the world of fallen mankind. He has revealed his judgments and his salvation. This salvation is announced and revealed stage by stage, to Adam, Noah, Abraham, Moses, Joshua, Samuel and to the later prophets. Having spoken by the prophets, God then spoke in a unique fashion by the incarnation of his Son whose life and ministry was later expounded in full by the apostles.

This subject of progressive revelation which we call biblical theology is important because it dictates our approach to the Bible as a whole. Writing in the *Encyclopaedia of Christianity,* Francis Anderson declares that, 'Biblical Theology is the most excellent of all studies, supreme over all other methods of setting forth the truth because it deliberately aims at remaining as close as possible to the method God himself has used in giving us his revelation.'[11]

When this biblical, theological method is applied in the case of Abraham we see that the covenant did not mean to him at that stage what is now fully revealed in the New Testament. Yet it is the constant error of Reformed non-Baptists to read the New Testament into the Old and having done that to equate the two, setting them up as equal together. They ignore and mutilate all the canons of biblical Theology in this matter for the simple reason that they begin with a steadfast determination to retain infant baptism.

Barton Payne in his work on this subject suggests that the covenant is the organising principle of biblical theology.[12] By that we understand him to mean that God's purpose in salvation, and in the forming of the Church, the bride of Christ, is announced and expressed in the form of a covenant. The unfolding and development of this covenant is one of the keys by which we can have a better grasp of the Bible.

Lest readers think that I am pressing this matter too hard let me describe the experience of a fellow Reformed Baptist pastor in America who attends a ministers' fraternal in his area in which all the ministers happen to be of Presbyterian persuasion. One day he challenged these men as to whether they regarded him as Reformed! Not one of them was prepared to do so, not because he does not believe all the doctrines of grace, but because he is a Baptist!

Now we need not behave like children and squabble about names. It does not matter too much if in a few isolated and backward areas Reformed Baptists are regarded as non-Reformed! What I hope to have achieved in these few pages is to prove that we have an enormous amount in common, the centralities of the faith which provide a solid basis for unity.

We do not wish to be like children and contend about names but if the subject is to be pursued then we will have to assert that it is we alone who believe on the covenant consistently and practice it faithfully—we are the true heirs of covenant theology! In this respect at least we are Reformed to the last detail.

Now it is my purpose to prove that Reformed Baptists give proper credence to the place, development and importance of the covenant. Not only do they do this in common with Reformed non-Baptists but they go further. Reformed Baptists alone do justice to the diversity of the administration of the covenant. Reformed Baptists alone are consistent in heeding the tremendous stress expressed in Hebrews chapters 8-10. They and they alone heed the double imperative to observe that the New Covenant has entirely replaced the Old, and that the Old as a way of practice or administration is now totally and completely revoked. Not so much as a stitch or particle remains. As a basis for practice it is utterly and completely done away with.

Reformed Baptists in this way are consistent in their practice. They alone are true and faithful to covenant theology as it respects the New Testament and baptism.

We have so much in common by which our unity is strengthened and our fellowship enriched yet when it comes to our churches there is a gulf. The difference between churches in which the membership is confined to those who maintain a credible and consistent confession of faith in lip and life, and churches where memberships are infiltrated by nominal believers, sometimes in large numbers, cannot be exaggerated.

The reformation of the sixteenth century has never been completed because the doctrine of Rome with respect to infant baptism was accommodated. Reasoning from the covenant was utilised for this accommodation.

We are concerned for Reformation in our day. Could any subject be more relevant or practical than that which directly controls the nature and constitution of the Church upon earth?

Practical Conclusions

Suppose an equal number of Reformed Baptists and Reformed non-Baptists, a dozen of each, lived in one specific geographic area, would that mean of necessity that two small separate churches would have to exist alongside one another? When those concerned have so much in common is it impossible to come to some agreement? Certainly unity would be facilitated if the essential differences be properly faced. It would help to observe:

1. That both sides accept covenant theology in every sense but differ over the implications of Hebrews Ch. 8.

2. That both sides are equally jealous about the bringing up of their children and applying to them all the advantages of the Christian Gospel.

3. That the great majority of Reformed non-Baptists accept the implications of original sin and reject presumptive regeneration.

4. That both sides recognise the futility of speculation about infant regeneration. Spurgeon, a Baptist, in sermon 411 takes a position that David Kingdon would not accept. Likewise Kuyper a Reformed non-Baptist takes a position his kinsman Douma would not accept.

5. If unity is to be feasible at the practical level a Church must take a definite position on baptism. This is because the practical implications are so far reaching. This can easily be seen in the chapter on that subject (Ch. 4) in the book *Local Church Practice* (Carey Publications). Nevertheless at the same time the extent of unity is so far reaching (if indeed both sides heartily accept the afore going exposition) that it would be scandalous not to co-operate to an extent commensurate with that unity.

6. The unity could possibly be expressed at the communion table but it is difficult to see how equal church membership can be compatible. The maintenance of two basically contradictory practices on Christian initiation is confusing to converts. I cannot see Baptists agreeing to the notion that we can take our choice when it comes to apostolic commandments.

On the other hand how difficult it is to persuade some Reformed non-Baptists that we are not neglecting our children in any way when we refuse to baptise them but rather dedicate them to God instead! For us dedication is for the entire period of their existence with us.

7. It will help when we come together if we can save time by not going over ground which has already been consolidated. It aids relationships all round when we are properly informed of the views of others.

8. Patience and forebearance in these matters is more pleasing to the Lord than the contrary. Any efforts to promote unity among believers is worthwhile.

[1] The 1689 section on the church has fifteen paragraphs in comparison to six in the Westminster. The Baptists grappled with responsibility to promulgate the Gospel and added a chapter, albeit a poorly defined one (Ch. 20). They omitted two chapters of the Westminster statement (30 and 31) and unhappily the concluding two paragraphs on marriage and divorce (Ch. 24).

[2] *The Reformers and the Theology of the Reformation*, William Cunningham, p. 1, Banner of Truth.

[3] cf. The Puritan view of the Early Church Council, Andrew A. Davies, Westminster Conference Papers for 1978.

[4] Documents of Vatican II, Austin P. Flannery, ed., Eerdmans, p. 733ff.

[5] *Christian Baptism*, John Murray, p. 59. *Believers and the Seed* by Herman Hoeksema, describes Kuyper's view in detail and then destroys it in no uncertain manner, p. 34ff. As Prof. Douma acknowledges Kuyper's teaching led to serious division in the Dutch Church. Hoeksema, a hyper-Calvinist, demolishes every form of presumption regarding children born to believers. He maintains the absolute free and sovereign grace of God in election. That is consistent. Who can argue with it?

[6] British and Foreign Evangelical Review, 1860, p. 939.

[7] British and Foreign Evangelical Review, 1860, p. 939.

[8] *Biblical Theology*, Chester K. Lehman, Vol. 1, p. 26, Herald Press. *Old Testament Theology*, Herman Schultz, Vol. 1, pp. 1 and 2, T. T. Clark, 1892. Lehman's work is the result of forty years tutoring in the subject. He is weak on the doctrines of grace and not always as firm in his rejection of liberal teachings as we would like.

[9] *Biblical Theology*, Geerhardus Vos, p. 13, Banner of Truth.

[10] *Theology of the Old Testament*, Oehler, p. 5, Klock and Klock.

[11] *Ency. of Christianity*, Vol. 2.

[12] *The Theology of the Older Testament*, Barton Payne, p. 71, Zondervan.

What is covenant theology?

2

COVENANT theology is associated with the Reformed faith because those in the Reformed tradition expounded in detail the subject of the covenant as it is unfolded in the Bible. God has from the beginning expressed his relationship with men in covenant terms.

The term covenant means a contract, pact or agreement between two parties. Grace means favour bestowed which is undeserved. The covenant of grace is that arrangement whereby God through grace alone has bound himself to save man from the just consequences of his sin.

The covenant of redemption (not to be confused with the covenant of grace) is an expression used to describe the provisions made within the Trinity for our salvation. It is wrong to assume that interest in the subject of covenant theology and the covenant of grace has been wholly confined to Calvinistic non-Baptist theologians. English Baptists found no reason to quarrel with the subject when they used the Westminster Confession as a basis for their own Confession published in 1689. In the next century John Gill was one of the sponsors to the publication in English of an extensive work on the covenants by the noted continental theologian, Herman Witsius. Baptists have sometimes been suspicious of covenant theology because it is employed by non-Baptists to accommodate infant-baptism.

It is true to say that non-Baptists have exercised a monopoly of covenant theology teaching, so much so that some 'Goliath-like' have tyrannised poor weak Baptists censuring them for their ignorance and always using the subject to endorse the error of infant-baptism. Some panic-stricken Baptists have been so foolish as to abandon covenant theology by adopting a false kind of dispensationalism—setting up the old covenant against the new. I venture a prophecy that when correctly handled covenant theology will be the best vindication of the Baptist position. Let us begin by viewing the subject in general.

The Bible is the story of how God has come to fallen man to reveal the way of salvation he has provided in his Son. The account begins with the creation and fall of man. Most theologians have spoken of a covenant of works made with Adam. Professor John Murray has challenged this idea and prefers to use the term 'The Adamic Administration' [1]. In pronouncing judgment on our first parents God also promised that through the woman would be born one who would gain victory over Satan. That is the first intimation or promise of salvation. Thereafter the idea of covenant or God binding himself to men is revealed progressively stage by stage.

The covenant of grace is one proceeding from its administrator, the one Triune God, with one purpose of salvation in mind. The covenant is revealed in a series of covenants which are related to each other. This relationship is one of development, each stage being preparatory to the next.

The principle of grace is evident with each covenant. In covenanting with men God never imposes upon them a system of earning their salvation. Even in the first instance of creation Adam and Eve had received everything needed for their happiness. They did not earn paradise. They were given paradise. All that was then required was an evidence or token of gratitude expressed by faithful, obedient submission in avoiding only one tree.

Having looked at the subject in general we will now examine the development of the covenant of grace. I have pointed to the unity of the covenant both in God its administrator and in its character of grace. The administration however at each stage reveals diversity. Different lessons are to be learned at each stage.

1. *The covenant made with Noah* (Genesis chapters 8 and 9)

This covenant was made with all creation or the cosmos. Noah's offering like all the sacrifices of the Old Testament typified or pointed to the great sacrifice of Calvary. Upon the basis of Christ's merit and Kingship God promised by covenant to preserve the whole world and provide all the basic needs of mankind until the end of time. This covenant of common grace is called common because it is such to all men and to all the creation. It was essential that mankind be preserved in order that the Gospel might be proclaimed to all. The fallen angels had no such provision of favour. They are reserved for judgment. In contrast our world is brimful of provisions for the benefit of mankind—all provisions of common grace. The Noahic covenant is universal and remains in operation to the end of time being different in that respect from the Mosaic covenant which is abrogated. The Noahic covenant is unconditional, no commandments being appended. What Professor Murray calls 'the divine monergism' is intensely exhibited—monergistic, meaning from one side, man contributing nothing.

2. *The covenant made with Abraham* (Genesis chapters 12, 15 and 17). The covenant made with Abraham was ratified by sacrifices. These confirmed the utter certainty of God's promise. Abraham had confirmed to him the promise of a seed—one in particular, that is the Messiah (Gal. 3:16; Gen. 13:15 and 17:8). Through one who would come out of Abraham all peoples of the earth would be blessed. To Abraham's progeny God promised the land of Canaan. Circumcision was given as a sign of keeping this covenant. While all males in the family and clan were to be circumcised this did not guarantee that all so circumcised would be included in its benefits. Ishmael, Jokshan, Midian and others (Gen. 25:2) were not included.

3. *The covenant made with Moses* (Exodus 19:5, 6). Through Moses as leader and mediator this covenant was made with the Hebrew nation and ratified by the blood of sacrifice (Ex. 24:8). Known as the Sinaitic covenant it was very comprehensive as to detail and became the central or main covenant of the Old Testament era. Therefore when we speak of the Old Covenant it is to the Sinaitic or Mosaic covenant that we refer. It is to that covenant expressly that the prophets like Jeremiah and Ezekiel refer, and it is that covenant to which the writer of the Hebrews epistle refers calling it 'The Old Covenant' (Heb. 8:8-13).

The Abrahamic covenant was fulfilled, assimilated into and confirmed by the Sinaitic covenant—fulfilled in land and people, assimilated as circumcision became a national seal, and confirmed as God pledged himself anew as the God of that chosen people of Abraham. Again it is important to note that this covenant is not a covenant of works but a covenant of grace. The ten commandments are founded on God's great act of redemption which was at the same time an act of mercy expressed in the opening words 'I am the Lord your God, who brought you out of Egypt, out of the land of slavery.' Now in order to please God and express their gratitude they were to keep his laws—not in order to be saved, but because they had been redeemed out of Egypt. God gave them his laws for their good and did not intend that they should exchange one form of slavery for another.

4. *The covenant made with David* (Psalm 89:3; 2 Sam. 7:13). By covenant, which is God's way of expressing an infallible certainty, the throne of David was guaranteed to be perpetual. This covenant like the others is messianic. One was promised who would come and occupy the throne of David and reign over God's people forever.

5. *The New Covenant.* The later prophets recognised that the central agreement, pact or covenant (that of Sinai) had been broken by Israel's unfaithfulness. Jeremiah affirmed this, foresaw the proof of it in the captivity of Babylon, and predicted the New Covenant (Jer. 31:31-34). Ezekiel surveyed God's covenantal dealings in an astonishingly vivid way and pointed to a new covenant (Ezek. 16). Like Jeremiah he predicted

the complete inward and spiritual nature of the new covenant (Ezek. 36: 24-28). Because of the inward change brought about by the new birth the faithfulness of God's people would be insured. The lack of this under the old covenantal administration was the main reason for the breakdown and ultimate dissolution of the Sinaitic covenantal relationship. Commenting on the new covenant Professor Murray says, 'The climax of redemption is the climax of covenant administration, and sovereign grace reaches the zenith of its manifestation and realisation. At the centre of all the covenants of redemptive grace was the promise, *I will be your God and ye shall be my people.* In this respect also the new covenant brings this relationship to the highest level of achievement, and there will be no further expansion or enrichment than that which the new covenant provides. Christ's blood secured its provisions; Christ is its mediator and surety. And He is the covenant. Nothing more ultimate is conceivable' [2].

6. The unity of the covenant seen in its development

Leading up to the finality of salvation provided in Christ are the preparatory stages and at each stage we can observe further enrichment of truth. First God preserved the earth in order to fulfil his purpose of redemption. Hence the Noahic covenant. God formed a special people to be the means by which he revealed himself first through the family of Abraham and then through the nation that came out of Abraham and which was led by Moses. Hence we read in Romans 3:2 that to this people the oracles or very words of God were entrusted. From their ranks the Messiah came. In Abraham the process of forming this nation and giving them a land was initiated. Israel was to be a unique people and circumcision was the sign and seal of that.

All this was confirmed in the Sinaitic covenant which has the same features as was used in pacts made between nations of those ancient times. There was the naming of the parties, the covenant history pointing back to Genesis and Abraham. The purpose of the covenant was stated and stipulations or obligations binding upon the people declared. There were the blessings if the pact was honoured and cursings if the pact was broken. There was sacrifice and there was the covenant meal (Exod. 24:9-11). Meredith Kline in his book *By Oath Consigned* describes the ancient forms of treaty or covenant between nations. Such information is very helpful and illustrative but should be in every way subservient to Scripture. What I mean is that the people of Israel submitted to the direct revelation of God in the establishment of a covenantal relationship and were not imitating the current national practices of those times. An example of a voluntary covenant typical of that age is the one between Jacob and Laban as recorded in Genesis 31:43-55.

In the Old Testament the spiritual aspect is contained within the protective shell of the external. This external shell falls away when we come to the

New Covenant for now all who form part of God's people know him, from the least to the greatest. All without exception have God's laws inscribed within them so that they love those laws.

We see that while there is unity, one God revealing one salvation, and progress step by step, there is also diversity. The administration of the Covenant is not the same in the New as in the Old. No chapter of Scripture highlights or emphasises this diversity more than Hebrews chapter eight. Here the difference between the old administration and that of the new is insisted upon. We must observe the progress from the Old to the New Covenants inasmuch as the spiritual aspect inherent within the Old becomes explicit in the New and is exhibited with a clarity which is in contrast to the Old.

The essential difference in the Covenants

What is the main difference between the covenants, Old and New? It is simply this that in the Old Covenant, qualification depended upon Hebrew status and descent. You had to be born physically into the Hebrew family to qualify and circumcision was the sign of inclusion. Of course proselytes or converts could enter but that was the exception not the rule. By contrast we find that with the New Covenant the qualification is repentance and faith irrespective of racial descent. Those who repent and believe irrespective of parenthood are those who are born again of the Holy Spirit (Jn. 1:12, 13). Expressly does the apostle declare that this is not of blood, nor of the will of man, nor of the will of the flesh. Not of human parenthood are people born again but by sovereign divine parenthood. That which is of the flesh is flesh (flesh can never rise higher than flesh) but that which is born of the Spirit is spirit (Jn. 3:6). A man must be born by the Father's calling, the Spirit's regeneration, and by fusion into or union with Christ, the reigning King.

Now there was fault found with the Old Covenant. That fault was that the disposition to keep it was lacking, lamentably lacking. That was unsatisfactory to say the least and it led ultimately to a breach of the covenant signified by the destruction of Jerusalem and the Temple, and the subsequent captivity in Babylon.

This fault with the Old Covenant was that Israel did not keep it. God repealed it to make place for the new (Heb. 8:7, 8). Note the fundamental and most obvious difference between the Old and the New, namely, that the new is NEW. It is brand new! It is pulsating with power and vigour because a risen victorious Christ is administering it so that every member of it is alive *in him*. We read in Hebrews chapters nine and ten of the wonderful fulfilment of salvation in the death, burial, resurrection and ascension of Christ. For instance we read, 'that by one offering he hath perfected forever them that are sanctified' (Heb. 10:14). That the New Covenant is New in contrast to the old is stressed by the emphasis placed in the Greek to describe the age or passing away of the old covenant administration. *Gēraskon* (v. 13) is the word used to describe it and means 'ageing into decay'. This leads to a further difference expressed by the term *aphanismou* which means to obliterate, destroy completely or wipe off the face of the earth.

As has already been explained we appreciate the unity of the covenants but not at the expense of the diversity of their administration, which diversity the Scripture insists upon. Both covenant administrations are one inasmuch as they are soteric, they have to do with salvation. Both are administered by the Trinity. But in the administration tremendous contrasts or difference are to be noted. Especially are these contrasts to be noted between the Abrahamic Covenant and the New Covenant. The differences can be observed as follows:

The Differences Between THE ABRAHAMIC COVENANT and the NEW COVENANT

1. Is old	Is new
2. Was initiatory (to be continued)	Is final
3. Was preparatory	Is complete
4. Was to be added to:	Cannot be added to:
(a) by the passover	is fulfilled in Christ
(b) by the Mosaic administration	is fulfilled in Christ
(c) by the Aaronic priesthood	is fulfilled in Christ
(d) by the Davidic covenant	is fulfilled in Christ
5. Is different in its subjects The Abrahamic covenant included:	
(a) All born into the family	All born of the spirit
(b) All belonging to the clan (nation)	Believers of all nations are now included (Gal. 3:28, 29).
(c) The flesh was first. New birth second	Now it is faith first and new birth first, not covenant status or human descent—John 1:12, 13.
(d) Only males received the sign	Now there is neither Jew nor Greek, slave nor free, male nor female— unity with Christ by faith is the only consideration—Gal. 3:28.
6. Is different in mode Administered in the flesh with a knife	Administered upon the whole body.
7. The spiritual meaning of circumcision became more clear with the unfolding of God's purposes.	The spiritual significance of baptism is immediately clear in the New Testament.
8. Embraced a physical land first with a better one in view later on— Gen. 17:8, Heb. 11:13	Embraces no special land in this world but only embraces the world to come.
9. Embraced one nation only.	Embraces all nations, tongues, and tribes—Rev. 5:9.
10. The contrast was between Israel and the Gentiles	The contrast is between the believing Church and the world.
11. Was revealed by theophany and sustained by periodic confirmation either by theophany as to Isaac, or by vision as to Jacob at Bethel	Is now applied directly by Jesus Christ exalted to supreme high-priesthood and mediatorship at God's right hand from which kingly position he administrates a whole set of immeasurably better and clearer promises.

12. The children born into this covenant such as the children of Leah and Rachel had the advantages of the covenant including its sign of circumcision	The children born into Christian households enjoy from the beginning the better promises mediated direct from Christ and held forth in the administration of the Gospel, a situation immeasurably superior to that of the children of Leah.
13. The sign and seal of the promises was given to all males on the 8th day—in hope of salvation	The sign and seal is given when the promises of salvation have been realised.
14. The sign was a sign of separation to a saviour to come (future)	The sign is a sign of separation into Christ who has now achieved all (past).
15. The receiving of salvation pointed to by circumcision might or might not be appropriated at a later date. But there was no further sign or seal given upon such appropriation. The only exception was that of Abraham himself. In that particular feature he was according to the express teaching of Paul the prototype of us all. Romans 4	The receiving of salvation is highlighted in the New Testament as the very glory of God's grace that gift being the result of sovereign grace (Eph. 2:1-10). A provision is made, which was not made in the covenant of Abraham or Moses, by which this glory can be celebrated in a magnificent way. Union with the glorious reigning Redeemer—living union with him in his death, burial, resurrection and present reign is celebrated by immersion.

By now my readers should be persuaded that we believe in the covenant grace, in its unity and diversity of administration from first to last. Through the administration of the covenant of grace in all its stages are lessons for our edification and comfort.

[1] *Collected Writings*, Vol. 2, p.49.
[2] *The New Bible Dictionary*, IVP, p.267.

Jesus and the little children

3

Eclipsing all other texts by way of use to support infant baptism is the account in the Gospels of the little children being brought to Jesus. The fullest account is that provided by Mark (10:13-16).

C. H. Spurgeon testified that this passage was employed against him more than any other in the great baptismal regeneration controversy which raged in 1864. That controversy began on Sunday morning June 5th when Spurgeon preached a sermon on Mark 16:15,16 showing that faith must of necessity precede baptism. At the same time he launched a devastating attack on the superstition of baptismal regeneration. He deplored the fact that Popery had made great strides in England. Such was the stir created by that sermon (no. 573) that eventually 350,000 copies were printed to satisfy the demand.

A few weeks later on 24th July, 1864, he preached on Mark 10:13-16 with the title, 'Children brought to Christ, not to the font.' It was in that sermon (no. 581) that he chose to expound on Mark 10:13-16 because of its usage against him. He showed that baptism has no place in that incident. It is our purpose to investigate the true meaning of the passage. There are three records of the incident, Mark 10:13-16, Matthew 19:13-15 and Luke 18:15-17. As already intimated the Marcan account is the most detailed:

> People were bringing little children to Jesus to have him touch them, but the disciples rebuked them. When Jesus saw this, he was indignant. He said to them, "Let the little children come to me, and do not hinder them, for the kingdom of God belongs to such as these. I tell you the truth, anyone who will not receive the kingdom of God like a little child will never enter it." And he took the children in his arms, put his hands on them and blessed them (Mark 10:13-15).

I will adopt the following procedure in opening up the subject. Firstly we will observe what the scholars say. Then we will see what the text has to say. Finally we will discuss briefly what is involved in a theology for children. The reason why we need to look at the scholars first is because ninety per cent of our commentaries use the passages referred to above to assert infant baptism. They simply assert it without going into detail so we have to spend a little time acquainting ourselves with a thought pattern which has become dominant.

1. *What the scholars say about Mark 10:13-16*

With good reasons Bishop J. C. Ryle is the most popular among the commentaries on the Gospels. He writes simply and practically. On Mark 10:13-16 he declares 'let us learn from this passage, *how much encouragement there is to bring young children to be baptised*'. (The italics are his.)

Hendriksen declares that our Lord's action shows that 'he definitely did not view them as "little heathen" who were living outside of the realm of salvation until by an act of their own they would join the church.' He goes on to say that 'since the little children of believers belong to God's church and to his covenant, baptism, the sign and seal of such belonging, should not be withheld from them'.

Lenski is severe in his condemnation of those who withhold baptism from infants. 'Who will count the crimes,' he says, 'that were thus perpetrated against helpless babes, even in the very name of Christ, by denying them the one divine means by which they can be brought and can come to their glorified Lord?' Little wonder that Lenski is passionate for he believes in baptismal regeneration which heresy is avoided by other infant-baptist writers. Nevertheless we will need to be sure of our ground in order to escape so severe a condemnation as committing a crime.

Jamieson, Fausset and Brown in their excellent commentary on the whole Bible published in clear print by Zondervan and distributed in the U.K. by E.P. choose the Lucan passage for exposition. The argument employed is that if the children are accepted by Jesus then what man can forbid water? However the suggestion is qualified by this thought, namely, that 'the infants must have been *previously brought to Christ himself* for his benediction.' The idea suggests that only the infants of Christian parents warrant the sign and seal of the benediction, that is to say the Lord's blessing, a blessing now symbolised in infant baptism. Thus in the space of the briefest paragraph the whole doctrine of infant baptism is erected. Matthew Henry argues along the same lines in his exposition of the Lucan passage and on Mark 10: 13-16 declares:

> It is true, we do not read that he baptised these children, baptism was not fully settled as the door of admission into the church, till after Christ's resurrection; but he asserted their visible church membership, and by another sign bestowed those blessings upon them, which are now appointed to be conveyed and conferred by baptism, the seal of the promise, which is *to us* and *to our children*. (His italics.)

Matthew Poole chooses to use the Matthean account for his comments and shows more caution than other expositors. Says he: 'We must take heed that we do not found infant baptism upon the example of Christ in this text, for it is certain he did not baptise these children. The argument is founded upon his words, not upon his practice.'

Our much esteemed non-Baptist readers will I am sure readily agree that I have been fair in my selection of quotes. Apart from Poole I have chosen statements which are most persuasive for infant-baptism.

Observation also must be made of those reasonings which employ the biblical theological approach (standing back and assessing revelation as it came progressively stage by stage) a procedure for which we have the warmest possible esteem and respect. However even that most enthralling way of expounding scripture requires scrutiny as it can easily be abused as we will now see.

Beasley Murray has shown that Wohlenberg in his commentary on Mark (in German) and Jeremias and Cullman in their writings on this subject argue that the whole section, Mark 10:1-31, provides a catechism instructing us how we are to frame our attitudes towards marriage, children and possessions. And so it is claimed that 'The second catechetical item, by implication, lays upon Christian parents the task and responsibility of bringing their children to Jesus, and that not in a general way but for the purpose of their receiving baptism.'[1]

Basically this reasoning is the same as that used by Matthew Henry except that it is enhanced by this notion of a little catechism (Mark 10: 1-31). This is only an idea, albeit an attractive one. Even if we accept it, it proves no more than the fact that we are to accept little children. Accepting them or blessing them does not mean that we have to baptise them.

One further argument should be mentioned which belongs to the science of language or semantics. On Mark 10:13-16 Oscar Cullman observes that the verb *hinder* is the same in Acts 8:36 (said the eunuch what *hinders* me to be baptised) as in Mark 10:14 (and *hinder* them not). Cullman suggests that the phrase 'what does hinder' had acquired a certain liturgical character in the primitive church, therefore for the Gospel narrators to use it implies that baptism is inferred in the case of the children. But the word 'hinder' is used in all kinds of situations and it is surely desperate reasoning which resorts to find its warrant for infant baptism on the basis of the mere usage of an expression.

2. *What the passage teaches*
The prominent elements of Mark 10:13-16 are:
(a) Here is an example of parents desiring the best for their children.
(b) Our Lord sets his seal upon such desires by blessing the children.
(c) As on other occasions (Matt. 18:1-9) our Lord did not hesitate to use children as an illustration of salvation.

(a) *Here is an example of parents desiring the best for their children*
Recounting a similar instance Luke says that the parents brought their babies to Jesus (Luke 18:15—*brephos:* infants) but Mark speaks of little children (*paedia:* little children). It seems obvious that little ones from babies in arms to small children are included.

The desire of obtaining the best for our children is universal. Our Lord adverted to the fact that we being evil give good gifts to our children. These people were of Hebrew stock who followed the custom of that time which was to seek the blessing of the synagogue rulers for their children. Apparently the synagogue ruler would lay his hands on the child's brow and pray. These parents sought such a blessing from the Prince of Peace who was illustrious among them for his powerful signs and wonders.

But these parents met with some strong resistance! The disciples were jealous for our Lord's time and did not regard these requests for children as worthy enough to break in upon more important work. They therefore requested the parents to move on. When there was reluctance on their part to get moving, the disciples like the world famous English police, resorted not to physical force but to authority by way of verbal command. They rebuked these parents for being a nuisance.

(b) *Our Lord sets his seal upon the desires of such parents*
When our Lord saw the parents and children being turned away he was indignant. The Greek word translated 'indignant' is a strong one meaning to be incensed, to be angry, or to be much weighed down. Our Lord corrected his disciples positively. 'Let them come to me': and negatively, 'do not hinder them.' He added a reason: the kingdom of heaven belongs to such. He then proceeded to enfold the infants or children in his arms one by one. He puts his hands upon them. He blessed them by which we understand that by prayer invoked the Father's favour upon them.

Observe that our Lord did not baptise them. There is no water or moisture in this passage, no, not so much as one solitary drop. As Spurgeon put it you might as well prove that he vaccinated them as prove that he applied water to them (sermon 581). In any case it is expressly declared that our Lord did not baptise (John 4:2).

Our Lord was himself a baptised person who confirmed the mission and authority of John the Baptist. He had joined the penitent sinners in going down into and coming up out of the waters of the river Jordan. In this way he identified himself with his people and united himself to them. In so doing he voluntarily took upon himself the role of substitute who would subsequently be immersed in a baptism of suffering. This identification of himself publicly as a sin-bearer received the audible approbation of the Father and the visible approval of the Spirit.

Baptism essentially involved cooperation. The person concerned is taken up with understanding, coming to, and submitting to the action of the baptiser in a sincere profession of 'turning to the Lord'. In the case of the little children and infants the ethos or scene is entirely different. They were brought to Jesus in the arms of the parents or guardians to be blessed. The concept of baptising therefore does not enter at all. The question was not one of baptism but of blessing. Baptism had its origins in the ablutions or washings of the Levitical order (Exod. 30: 17-21, Is. 1: 16ff., Jer. 4: 14, Ezek. 36: 25 and Zech. 13: 1), in proselyte baptisms and finally in the unique baptisms of John which were preparatory and basic to Christian baptism. Blessing little ones had its origin in the custom of the times. Nor should this custom be confused with circumcision which took place for males only eight days after birth.

The practice then was *not* one pertaining to circumcision for male infants eight days old or of dipping and washing of repentant sinners but of blessing.

We know that John's baptism was an immersion signifying repentance and that Christian baptism is an immersion into water signifying union of the candidate with the Father, Son and Holy Spirit symbolising his regeneration thereunto and the washing away of his sins henceforth to walk in newness of life. But what then was this blessing of the babes? We find the answer in the synagogue custom of those times. The synagogue rulers prayed for and laid their hands upon the children brought to them.[2] This is documented by H. L. Strack and P. Billerbeck.[3]

Looming in our minds is the question, what did this blessing mean? What did it procure for the little ones? The Greek word used in Mark 10: 18 (*eulogeo*) is the common word meaning simply to speak well of. It is found some 450 times in the Septuagint (the Greek translation of the Old Testament). In most cases the translation is of the Hebrew word *barak* (bless) which means to invoke or to seek God's favour for others.

It would appear that there are two types of blessing.

Firstly there is the instance of a blessing being unconditional and irrevocable which was the case when blind Isaac conferred the blessing on Jacob who deceived him and stole the blessing from his first born brother Esau. In that case there was only one inheritance to bestow and only one line by which the Messiah could come. We can see therefore why the blessing was irrevocable.

Secondly there was a general blessing which can be defined as the desire to grasp hold of the means of grace and make them effectual. The question concerning the Lord and the little children is whether he simply prayed for their wellbeing or whether he actually dispensed blessing in an infallible and irrevocable sense? Could those parents then go home with the absolute assurance that their children would be saved because Jesus had blessed them? There is nothing to support that view. The little ones were not being blessed in the sense that Jacob was blessed by Isaac. Rather the sense is the same as that of Numbers 6:24-26 which was blessing invoked by the priests upon the people in general which blessing was a reminder to them that through submission of themselves to the Lord such blessings would be secured. It would appear that this was the case with the parents and the children. By coming to Jesus they were coming to the right and only source of blessing and salvation. As we have seen the custom of the times was for parents to secure benedictions for their children from the rabbis.

The word 'he blesses them' is linear rather than punctiliar. It is not a blessing once and for all, which is punctiliar like a fullstop. Rather it is linear or ongoing. If they came again the next year he would bless them again. People tend to think of having their children 'done' and that's it! Fullstop! That is the reason why some parents, if they do not have their children 'done' in infant baptism like to have them 'done' in infant dedication in a church service. Millions have had their children 'done' who have never thought to bless those children with the true blessing of ongoing constant Gospel nurture and instruction.

Everywhere, whether we look into Deuteronomy six or Ephesians six, the stress is upon parental responsibility to bring their children up in the full nurture of instruction backed by constant prayer and godly living and example. Never are parents encouraged to put their trust in anything else for their children but the grace of God as he may be pleased to use the means of grace. John the Baptist stressed that in no way at all are we to look to or rely upon blood descent for salvation. '*Do not even begin to think to yourselves we have Abraham as our Father*' (Matt. 3:9. Note the aorist subjunctive *dozēte* 'do not even let it enter your mind').

To summarise then our Lord vindicates all parents who bring their children to him for he is the only source of salvation. The blessing is not a once and for all thing but rather we are taught by the passage that we must never cease to bring our children to Jesus. If these parents or guardians returned the very next day the disciples would not be allowed to chase them away. We too must be ready to receive children always. We must attend to their needs and guide them. However young they may be they should be included in our prayers. At all stages of their upbringing they are to be nurtured by their parents and by the church and ministry. Preachers do best who always remember the young ones in the congregation and instruct and exhort them simultaneously with the adult hearers.

(c) *Our Lord did not hesitate to use children as an illustration of salvation*
'I tell you the truth,' said Jesus, 'anyone who will not receive the kingdom of God like a little child will never enter it' (Mark 10:15).

The emphasis here is on receiving the kingdom of God like a little child. Children are as full of sin as adults only the potential for that sin has not had time to develop. Children are also proud. Even tiny children will pout and sulk if their pride is hurt. Our Lord in no way nullifies the emphatic Biblical doctrine of original sin. He is drawing our attention to something which is true of all children throughout the world. What is that? It is that children are naturally receptive. They are not intellectually sophisticated. For instance they do not stumble at accounts of the supernatural and of miracles. Children will accept the account of creation in six days without problems.

How immensely difficult it is to gather a congregation of adult hearers— how easy to gather a group of little ones. This does not mean that the conveying of a Biblical truth to a receptive child regenerates that child. How easy it would be for us all if that was the case! But nobody will deny the natural receptivity of little ones is great compared to adults who will invent a thousand and one excuses and fabrications to condone their unbelief. I contend then that it is the intellectual simplicity and humility of a little child that our Lord refers to. This is a humility which knows nothing of the ambitious scheming of the worldly-wise who plot and plan for their own aggrandisement. It is the humility of simplicity which knows nothing of ambitious self seeking. This surely is the characteristic recommended by our Lord. H. B. Swete says, 'it is not so much the innocence of young children that is in view, as their spirit of trustful simplicity'.[4]

Let us look at the incident recorded in Matthew:

At that time the disciples came to Jesus and asked, 'Who is the greatest in the kingdom of heaven?' He called a little child and had him stand among them. And he said: 'I tell you the truth, unless you change and become like little children, you will never enter the kingdom of heaven. Therefore, whoever humbles himself like this child is the greatest in the kingdom of heaven. And whoever welcomes a little child like this in my name welcomes me' (Matt. 18:1-5).

The outstanding feature of the passage cited is the absolute necessity of receptivity and faith. It is intellectual pride that prevents people from hearing or obeying. We regularly observe this in open air preaching. Adults are ashamed to listen. If they are drawn then they prefer to listen in some secluded spot where they are unlikely to be detected by others. Note also the concluding sentence about welcoming little children which endorses the substance of Mark 10:13-16 that we are to receive children, instruct them in the Gospel and guide them to Christ.

A theology of children

This is a large subject which we will only look at briefly.

To be born into a Christian family is to be born into an environment of blessing. To be born into or to be adopted into such a family is to be sanctified in the basic meaning of that term. To be sanctified simply means to be set aside or apart. Hence the unconverted partner in a marriage is set apart. He is sanctified only in the sense that God takes into account the fact that he or she is joined in life to a believer. That does not mean that that person is holy in the converted sense. 1 Corinthians 7:14 expressly states the case of the unbelieving partners, 'they are holy'. Their lives are the very opposite of holiness. It is their position of being set apart that is acknowledged. Now the same applies to all children born into a Christian family. To be born into the arena of New Covenant living (an expression to be enlarged on presently) is to be privileged indeed. That is why the word sanctified or holy is used in 1 Corinthians 7: 14. As baptism is not warranted in the case of the unbelieving partner so it is not warranted with unbelieving children.

Prayer and teaching are the means used by the Holy Spirit to bring about regeneration but such means do not automatically guarantee regeneration. To bless children therefore is consistent with the privileges already surrounding them. Such prayers or blessings endorse and strengthen those privileges. Such blessing of the means of grace is in order that the grand object of baptism into the Trinity becomes a living reality and when that is accomplished by grace then follows the appropriate season for rejoicing in water baptism.

Reference has been made to being born into the arena of New Covenant living. The Dutch scholar J. Geertsema in a theological address in 1978 put forward a thesis that the Sermon on the Mount was the proclamation of the King or the Messenger of the New Covenant. His reasons are convincing. He points out that the structure of the Sermon on the Mount is covenantal in character being similar in some structural features to the Mosaic covenant as expressed in Exodus chapters 19-24 or in the book of Deuteronomy. I do not want to digress now with details why I believe that this approach has a great deal to commend it but simply point out that it raises that oration of Christ to the fitting height of majesty and kingship that it deserves far above the grovelling moralising that has characterised so much teaching on the Sermon on the Mount. This is the proclamation of the King of kings *to his disciples* who alone have the power to understand and practise the laws which God writes on their hearts. He alone as king has the power to confer the new earth to his citizens. The second clauses in the beautitudes so often left unexplained are seen in a new light when related to the mediator of the new covenant.

Now children born into Christian families are born into the arena of Covenant living. Their parents are heirs of the kingdom of heaven, love the truth of God, are pure in heart and are peacemakers. They are the salt of the earth and the light of the world (Matt. 5:1-16). They understand and reflect the spiritual inward demands of God's holy law as explained by our Lord (Matt. 5:17-36). They appreciate that the purpose of Christ in the new covenant is to make his people children of our heavenly Father and that all new covenant life is lived with the motive of pleasing the Father because we are his children (Matt. 6).

Into such an arena children of believers are born. To understand that spiritual world into which they are born they themselves must be born again. Such new birth is not by blood nor by ritual, nor by sprinkling, nor by 'being done' either in a dedication or by a washing. We are born again by the word of truth. The blessing is the blessing of nurture which on an average lasts for twenty years. That tremendous responsibility, the responsibility of securing the true blessing that is in Christ for our children is what is being stressed in the incident of the little ones being brought to him.

Such a conclusion is consistent with the entire Biblical testimony. Matthew Poole was right to show caution about infant baptism and Mark 10:13-15. William L. Lane in his scholarly commentary on Mark[5] repudiates any basis for seeing infant baptism in the incident of Jesus and the little children.

Let us bring our children to Jesus at all times that through his blessing of the practical means appointed, they may be established in the Faith.

[1] *Baptism in the New Testament*, G. R. Beasley Murray, p. 322.
[2] *Commentary on Mark*, H. B. Swete, p. 220. Swete cites Hastings, D. B., iii, p. 84ff. to document benedictions obtained from rabbis. [3] Vol. 1, pp. 807f., vol 2, p. 138.
[4] Ibid., p. 221. [5] *Mark*, New London Commentary, M. M & S. 1974, p. 360.

Various views of non-Baptists considered

4

IN the Old Covenant the Jews were taken by God's hand and led out of Egypt to become God's one and only nation upon this earth. That nation was monolithic in as much as every person born into it was included in the Covenant made by God with Moses. Within that body of people was to be found a spiritual body. In Isaiah's day the spiritual body had shrunk to about a tenth and by the time of Jeremiah and Ezekiel the number of the spiritual had further declined to a very tiny remnant. It is remarkable to observe how God revived the small nucleus that survived in Babylon after the shattering invasion of 587 B.C. From that time onward the principle of inward renewal or regeneration is especially brought to the fore by the prophecies in preparation for the impending New covenant administration which completely displaced the Old.

We have already outlined the differences between the Abrahamic covenant and the New covenant. It will help to have a summary of some of these before us now.

Old Covenant	*New Covenant*
Inclusion was by birth or covenant status the sign of which was circumcision which pointed to the necessity of regeneration.	Inclusion is by a new heart (regeneration), the evidences of which are repentance and faith.
Spiritual nurture was by a sacrificial system and a priesthood to administer it, together with the teaching of prophets.	Spiritual nurture is mainly by the ministry of the Word in preaching and also by fellowship with the Lord's people. All believers are priests and all believers have access at all times to God's throne of grace.
A variety of sacrifices was made by the priests which pointed to God's provision of an atonement.	Only one sacrifice is commemorated, namely the perfect sacrifice of Christ once and for all. This Passover is remembered round the Lord's Table.

Membership was registered in families and tribes: Judah, God, Manasseh, Levi, etc.	Membership is of individuals with a local body of believers in which discipline is maintained by elders recognised and set apart according to the Scriptures.
Discipline was maintained by elders. Grievous sin or apostasy was punishable by death.	Discipline is maintained by elders. Reproof, exclusion from the Lord's Table, suspension from membership and ultimately excommunication are the means of discipline.
Children were included in the body from birth. The sign of circumcision was given to males on the eighth day, a mark in their flesh that they belonged to the nation of Israel. Providing they did nothing outrageous they were always part of the Jewish nation even though they might never show any spirituality whatever. No suggestion is ever made of excluding groups such as the Sadducees who rejected the doctrine of the resurrection.	Children of believers are included from the time of birth in the nurture and teaching of the church, enjoying all the benefits of the means of grace. When the central promise of the New Covenant is evidenced in repentance and faith (knowing the Lord), then individual members born into Christian homes are baptised and welcome into formal membership.

Now having observed some differences let us survey some of the viewpoints and conclusions come to by those who practice infant baptism. It would take an extended study just to present the differences of view in Holland let alone survey all the positions held. My purpose at this stage is to illustrate the confusion that exists. Noteworthy is the salient feature that all non-Baptists neglect or avoid the Hebrew 8: 6-13 insistence on a *new* administration. It is a *New* Covenant and 'Not according to the covenant that I made with their fathers.' The words NOT ACCORDING TO THE OLD COVENANT (Jer. 31: 32) ought to be written in letters of shining gold, and hung over every baptismal font. The great or cardinal difference between the Old and the New is that in the New Covenant a new heart and spirit must be given. Regeneration is the prerequisite. Without regeneration a person cannot know the Lord. To belong or to be included you must know the Lord, as it says, *'for they will all know me from the least of them to the greatest of them'* (Heb. 8: 11).

1. The Roman Catholic position

Roman Catholics believe in baptismal regeneration. This automatically secures the forgiveness of all past sins. They believe that the rite is absolutely necessary to salvation and that it is not possible for newly-born infants to be saved unless they are baptised. The Trent Catechism declares, 'Infants unless regenerated unto God through the grace of baptism, whether their parents be Christian or infidel, are born to eternal misery and perdition.' However this idea has been moderated and another realm invented. This is the place called *limbus infantum* a place of non-suffering where unbaptised infants are sent.

If we were to take this teaching seriously we might conclude that 93% of the population of the Republic of Ireland are regenerate since 93% are

R.C. and baptised. Likewise we would expect 93% of the population of Italy to be regenerate and 95% of Poland.

To read the documents of Vatican II shows that the Catholics have moderated their outlook considerably. There are many contradictions in these documents. For instance on page 365 we are led to believe that baptism into the Roman Catholic church is essential to salvation and without it nobody can be saved. However later on page 469 in dealing with the 'decree on ecumenism' it is made plain that Christians of other communities are acceptable and that section there is a further assertion that rebirth is through the rite of baptism even though it is administered in other communities. With the casuistry for which the Catholics are so well known we suppose that they could get round these contradictions by saying that damnation belongs to those who know the church of Rome is correct and yet rebel against it. We suppose furthermore that they would regard those outside Rome as being ignorant and therefore needing to be subject to better instruction.

The Roman Catholic doctrine of regeneration is not consistently maintained because their teaching makes it plain that many grow up not to adhere to the faith and therefore are lost. A proper understanding of the doctrine of regeneration means that once regenerate a person can never be lost.

2. The position of Dr. Abraham Kuyper

Dr. Kuyper was a great theologian and author of a three volume classic on common grace. He left the ministry to enter politics and eventually became the prime minister of the Netherlands. He elaborated a most peculiar teaching about baptism. Dr. Kuyper taught that 'at the very moment when the minister administers the water of Baptism, your Mediator and Saviour performs a work of grace in the soul of the baptised child'.[1] This mark of grace is the grace of regeneration. But the teaching which follows is very subtle because Dr. Kuyper was careful to point out that when the results of this regeneration are not forthcoming we must presuppose that it is really there but hidden away in the subconscious. According to Kuyper this hidden grace of regeneration should appear at some future time, perhaps even seventy or eighty years later. We can imagine troubled parents calling in their pastor to deal with the tantrums of a wicked, disobedient son.

'We thought he was born again when you baptised him,' say they, 'but he blasphemes Christ and will not obey his parents!' 'Never mind,' says the pastor reassuringly, 'you must regard him with patience as a believer and faithful member of the church because in due course that secret regeneration hidden in the sub-consciousness will come to the surface.'

This is the famous presupposed regeneration teaching of Kuyper which writers like Hoeksema expose as erroneous.

3. *The position of Dr. Charles Hodge*

As we would expect this eminent Presbyterian theologian based his teaching on the old covenant. It would be too laborious to follow the process of thought for each writer. The reasoning in each case is similar but the conclusions differ. Hodge taught that in baptising infants we bring them to salvation and write their names in heaven. However he taught that it was possible for these same children afterwards to erase their names from the Lamb's book of Life. Let us view his words well:

> Do let the little ones have their names written in the Lamb's book of life even if they afterwards choose to erase them; being thus enrolled may be the means of their salvation.[2]

Now we must allow for the license of illustration, namely, that he means that infant baptism is a means of grace. Nevertheless even when we have done that we are still amazed! Are we really to believe that parents have the power to put their children's names in the Lamb's book of Life, and later that those children have power to erase them again. Even Arminius would shudder to think that such power could be attributed to man!

4. *The position of Prof. W. Heyns*

Prof. Heyns taught theology at Calvin College in America for a number of years and his teaching on baptism had considerable influence.

Prof. Heyns developed a scheme in which we are to understand that by baptising infants grace is infused into them whereby, to quote the Professor, 'they receive a certain life, a life which is not indeed the life of regeneration, but nevertheless life. Through this life they are put in a position to take possession of and to accept the offered promise, the essence of the covenant, or reject it'.[3]

Well here is an amazing proposition for by sprinkling the little ones we create a third race, a race of little Arminians who grow up with free-will to accept or reject offered grace! There is the race of Adam into which we are all born. We know too of the race of the second Adam, that is Christ, into which we have to be born by the Holy Spirit. But nowhere in Scripture do we find the existence of a third race of people who are partially liberated and who by water and upbringing possess a special spiritual discernment or freedom to choose or reject the Gospel.

5. *The position of Herman Hoeksema*

Hoeksema is an out and out hyper-Calvinist who categorically rejects the doctrine of common grace and gives no quarter whatever for the free offers of the Gospel.[4] Nevertheless his uncompromising hold on the doctrine of election preserves him from all the aforegoing errors. The sovereign right of God to choose some and reject others irrespective of any other factors is correctly maintained by Hoeksema. He recognises that the doctrine of election ensures that God is by no means obligated to save the children of believers. He was not so obligated in the Old Testament administration and now he is not so obligated in the New. Salvation is not by blood, nor by the will of the flesh but by the sovereign will and choice of God. This exercise of sovereign grace is absolute. Therefore we are in no position to guarantee the salvation of any individual on the grounds that he or she was born into a Christian household. Hoeksema is correct in his firm assertion of this principle. He expounds what he calls 'the organic idea in Scripture'. Summed up in a sentence this means simply that God does work in families—the Hebrew family of the Old Testament and now in believing families in the New. God who predestinates souls to salvation also predestinates the means to that end. To be born into a Christian household is to be born with the means of salvation. Following this 'organic' idea we see that the Lord worked in the family of Seth (Gen. 4: 25, 26) and the families of Noah and Abraham. Afterwards he worked in the nation of the Jews. We see also how he worked in Timothy's family, in his grandmother Lois and in his mother Eunice (2 Tim. 1: 5). In our day we continue to observe the principle. Grace has run in some of our families for three or four generations.

As with the other positions outlined, Hoeksema rests the practice of infant baptism firmly and squarely on the Old Testament dispensation. But he observes that all born into the Jewish nation were circumcised though not necessarily saved. Now all born into Christian families must on the same principle be baptised but this too in no way guarantees salvation.

Hoeksema represents a large school of Reformed non-Baptists who observe the unity of the Old Covenant administration with the New but fail to observe the clearly enunciated differences of administration between the two (Heb. 8: 6-13).

Hoeksema points out how the principle of election is asserted very strongly in Romans chapter nine. Both Jacob and Esau were circumcised yet Jacob was chosen and Esau rejected. The same observation can be made with regard to Isaac and Ishmael. Both were circumcised but Isaac alone was the son of promise. We could go further and presume that all twelve sons of Jacob were circumcised. Yet one after the other they grew up to manifest the evil of their unregrenerate hearts. Simeon and Levi were cruel, ruthless murderers. Reuben was guilty of an incestuous relationship and Judah of adultery. All the brothers with the exception of Reuben and Benjamin conspired to destroy Joseph and in the event compromised and sold him as a slave instead. Afterwards they willingly imposed the most appalling heartbreak upon Jacob by maintaining their miserable deception about Joseph's death.

If the situation is the same in both Old and New Covenant dispensations then we must expect that whether baptised or not children born into Christian households are going to grow up in an unregenerate state.

Not all the water of the Pacific or Atlantic oceans can change the fact that flesh is flesh. Nor can we control the Holy Spirit with a ceremony. He blows where he wills and when he wills.

6. *The position of Professor John Murray*

In contrast to Herman Hoeksema who teaches that we must regard the visible church as consisting of a mixture of elect and reprobate, Professor John Murray teaches that we must regard all baptised infants of Christian parents as regenerate, that is until they prove otherwise. Says Professor Murray 'Baptised infants are to be received as the children of God and treated accordingly.'[5]

The professor then quotes the Westminster Assembly's Directory for Public Worship which Directory makes it very plain that this whole idea is based firmly upon the Abrahamic Covenant of the Old Testament. This was the line of thought followed by Calvin and which was formulated in Reformed creeds such as the Belgic Confession and the Heidelberg Catechism.

We come now to make some concluding observation as follows.

1. *The need for clear understanding of the doctrine of regeneration*

We can see from some of the aforegoing views that great theologians like Kuyper and Hodge feel that baptism must really signify regeneration. To them it must mean that and so they make it to mean that. In response we see the need to understand what the new birth really is. Professor Murray in his book *Redemption Accomplished and Applied* reminds us that regeneration is 'nothing less than a new creation by Him who calls the things that be not though they were'. He also reminds us of Ezekiel 36: 26 'A new heart also will I give you, and a new spirit will I put within you.' The new birth takes place in a moment of time and once a man is a new creature in Christ Jesus he can never be anything else but that. C. R. Vaughan declares of the new birth, 'It makes a man a new creature in Christ; renews his nature; it recolours his character; it transforms his will; it remoulds his whole system of thinking, feeling, and acting. It gives him new objects to live for; new rules to live by; new principles to impel to action; and new sensibilities to success or failure in the progress and development of that new life.'[6]

While regeneration is inward and hidden it is a work of omnipotence and the effects of an almighty work are to be seen. Resurrection begins inside and immediately results in life. Lazarus came out of his tomb. Paul quit breathing slaughter and began to pray.

The new birth is the first resurrection (Eph. 2: 1-10, Rev. 20: 6). In short the new birth is a mighty supernatural work of God whereby he makes a bad tree into a good tree.

The power with which this is done is compared to the power which raised our Lord Jesus Christ from the dead (Eph. 1:19,20). This reminds us that God uses the Scriptures and preaching to bring dead souls to life. It is through his Word that he brings the new birth to pass (Jas. 1:18, 1 Pet. 1:21,22).

In the light of all this it is erroneous to reduce the evidence of regeneration to something so passive that they cannot be recognised. Essentially the New Testament church consists of those who are the recipients of the New Covenant blessing of a new heart and a new spirit, that is regeneration. Every local church worthy of the name operates on this vital principle that it is composed of people who know the Lord because he has put them in Christ Jesus who has become for them wisdom from God—that is their righteousness, holiness and redemption.

A sure way to have a dead, formalistic, nominal, lifeless church is to follow Dr. Kuyper's teaching on presuppositional regeneration which is a dangerous delusion—a world of make-believe. Little wonder that so many Reformed non-Baptists in the Netherlands have rejected that error.

2. The necessity to maintain a proper doctrine of original sin

Our Lord in speaking to a privileged child of the Old Covenant, Nicodemus, not only insisted on the necessity of the new birth, that is for Nicodemus, but also reminded him of the fundamental principle that 'that which is born of the flesh is flesh and that which is born of the spirit is spirit' (John 3:6). Everyone without exception is born out of Adam, is guilty of his first sin and is destitute of that original righteousness in which he was created. Moreover all are born with the corruption of Adam's fallen nature. Without exception all so born are by nature hostile to God and spiritual truths and at the same time wholly determined to serve themselves and this world. There can be no compromise about the enmity which is incipient in every child of Adam. All the sprinklings in the world do not make the slightest difference to this basically unspiritual and evil nature. It is true that children born into Christian households are not pagans in the sense that they do grow up under Gospel teaching. This privilege and knowledge does not however change in the slightest their basic disposition of alienation from the living God. What was true of the religious child of the covenant, Nicodemus, is true of them, 'You must be born again!'

3. The necessity of a right attitude toward our children

Jeremiah who worked within the Old Testament covenant community declared emphatically that, 'the heart is deceitful above all things and beyond cure. Who can understand it?' The effects of a godly upbringing can be the cause of our children being well behaved, polite and affable. These are wholesome and attractive characteristics but until they are born again they will have no disposition and motivation to live for the glory of God and in vital communion with him. They may learn to say prayers, read the Bible and participate in various Christian activities but all this still falls short of 'knowing the Lord'.

Indeed it is much more difficult to awaken young people who have become persuaded that all is well with them because of their privileges. At any time it is the hardest thing on earth to awaken desperate sinners to their awful condition and plight. But I would say that it is even more difficult than that to awaken sinners who feel no need because they are surrounded by good things and by a false complacency that all is well with them because they observe religious practices and because they are not guilty of any shocking sins. To hide the real condition of a person's soul is to ignore the most important reason why the new birth is indispensible.

Because they accept the awful realities of original sin Baptists concentrate wholly upon the means of grace provided by God. It takes all the spiritual artillery we possess to awaken people out of their self-righteous complacency to be brought to see that they are hell-deserving sinners. This applies to our own off-spring just as much as it does to those outside. As in physical warfare all the forces, army, navy and air force, are to be called up into total all-out commitment and effort. So in our spiritual warfare all the means of grace provided by God must be employed.

The worst possible thing that we can do is to lull our children into the idea that they are already regenerate when there is no valid evidence for this. On the contrary in our prayers, teachings, church services, fellowship, the helpful occasions such as visiting preachers, the proper use of special events such as Christian house-parties, the love, care and concern of fellow members of the church, the encouragement of the officers of the church, the right use of family worship, all backed up with godly living in the home and family discipline, all these means are to be wholeheartedly employed in bringing up our children in the nurture and admonition of the Lord. We are to look to him and implore him to bring them to faith even as we ourselves have been brought out of spiritual deadness by regeneration to a lively faith and repentance from our sins.

[1] *Believers and their Seed* by Herman Hoeksema (henceforth abbreviated as H.H.), p. 36.
[2] *Systematic Theology* volume 3, p. 588.
[3] cf. pp. 70-75 *Essays on the Covenant of Grace* quoted from H.H., p. 19.
[4] H.H., p. 126ff.   [5] *Christian Baptism*, p. 59.   [6] *The gifts of the Holy Spirit*, p. 188.

Appendix 1

The testimony of the word 'baptism' as a metaphor

A metaphor is a figure of speech in which a word or phrase literally denoting one kind of object or idea is used in place of another to suggest a likeness or analogy between them. For example Christ is called 'a vine', 'a rock', 'the door' and 'the lamb'. The Church is called a bride, a building and a body. Satan is called 'a great dragon' and 'that ancient serpent'. An example of action is that believers are living stones being built into a temple (1 Pet. 2:4).

There are outstanding metaphorical uses of the word 'baptism' in which we do not claim that water closed in around the whole bodies of the people involved or, in fact, that water of any kind — mist, cloud or drops touched their bodies at all.

Our Lord was baptized in sufferings. The word is used in a metaphorical way. He was baptized in his own blood. The reason why baptism is used is precisely because it conveys the meaning of being overwhelmed. It conveys the sense of completeness and totality.

The word is also used in 1 Corinthians 10:2. All the children of Israel were baptized into Moses in the cloud and in the sea. To look down on that scene from a helocopter might well have revealed the water being held back in the form of a gigantic coffin or funeral casket. The water did in fact drown Pharaoh and become a coffin for him and his army.

The meaning brought out in the context is that through this overwhelming experience of exodus and salvation from the chariots of Pharaoh, the children of Israel were born as a nation, an experience in which they were united or wedded to their leader, Moses. It should not escape our attention that the redemption was by blood — a blood redemption of the Passover Lamb. They had passed out under doorposts sprinkled with the blood of lambs, and by the same token, were seen safely through the seas of destruction. The reference 'in the sea and in the cloud' is included to emphasize the unity of the people in protection from the sea and from the Egyptians by the cloud which in Exodus 14:19, 20 is described as moving from the front of the host of Israel to the rear. The cloud became darkness to the Egyptians but light to the Jews. The whole episode was one single act of omnipotent salvation — a baptism! A nation was initiated. A nation was born. It was a nation with Moses as their head. The parallel is obvious. In baptism the convert is initiated. He is born into a new world not with Moses but with Christ as his head, not with the Mosaic law but with the Gospel administration as his rule of life. At the same time, the baptism of a believer denotes the closest possible joining to Christ, a union with Christ in his death and resurrection which is utterly essential to salvation.

In 1 Peter 3:20, 21 we have another use of baptism in a metaphorical sense. The ark is like Christ. Noah's household, eight people in all, came through the deluge to be the heirs of a new world. It was an overwhelming experience and as in the previous two cases cited we could not use the terms 'sprinkling' or 'pouring' as metaphors, as those terms would be meaningless and hence ridiculous. Peter uses baptism as a figure to describe what happened in Noah's case, and then he turns to the Christians and reminds them that they have a similar figure in believer's baptism in water. They too have come through the waters of destruction, but in their case a washing did take place, a washing away of sin by which their consciences are now clean. Says the believer: Christ was once offered to bear the sins of many. He has borne away all my sin. That was portrayed in my baptism in which the merits of his death were made over to me.

We need never get confused about contact of water on the bodies of the escaping Israelites or on the bodies of Noah's family. Because baptism bears so powerful a meaning it alone can provide the needful metaphors in the three cases cited, Christ's suffering, the ark and the Red Sea. This metaphorical use of the word in no way removes the reality of our Lord going physically into the waters of baptism, and likewise of all believers being submerged in a burial, and in the washing of their whole bodies (Rom. 6:1-4; Heb. 10:22).

A final and inescapable observation is that baptism is always used to describe a major, or cataclysmic event. Whether believer's immersion, or the flood, or escape through the Red Sea by a nation, or Christ immolated on the Cross — it is always an event *maximus,* never *minimus.* Nothing could be more inappropriate than a few drops of water to signify so great an event as escape from eternal hell by complete union with Christ in his superlative saving acts.

Appendix 2

Historical perspective on the literature of baptism

Very few of the books to which I shall refer are now in print and for that reason I will not attempt to give any details other than that of the titles and sometimes I will refer to authors only.

E. Brooks Holifield in *The Covenant Sealed* outlines the debate on baptism among the Puritans. As early as 1622 the Baptists were seen as a threat. The weakness of the non-Baptist position was soon detected by the contradictory arguments put out. Samuel Ward of Sidney Sussex College, Cambridge adopted a position similar to that held by Prof. Douma that infant baptism does actually save the infants. Most other Puritan divines were embarrassed by Ward's position. Under pressure Ward developed a doctrine to the effect of sustaining a regeneration strong enough to save infants if they died in infancy but inadequate later.

The tension between the non-Baptists seems always to be between those who say that baptism is just a sign and nothing more and those who wish to make it more than that, either by an infusion of some kind of grace or else by a legal right conferred in the constitution of the infants as Christians and members of the church, even if not regenerated.

Another Puritan, Burges, elaborated a principle similar to that taken up by Abraham Kuyper. This was that initial regeneration takes place with the sprinkling. Full regeneration is actualized at a later date.

In 1643 John Tombes attempted to persuade a special committee of the Westminster Assembly of the error of infant baptism. Tombes could not bear the thought of separation and therefore never joined the Baptists formally.

At that time Richard Baxter strongly defended infant baptism. In his early ministry Baxter doubted infant baptism so much that he discontinued the practice. Later in defending infant baptism he proposed very tentatively that sprinkling conferred the power to obey God. That is more or less the position elaborated by Prof. Heyns of Calvin Seminary this century.

John Owen was one of those who took up his pen to defend infant baptism against the exposures of Tombes. His treatise (*Works* vol. 16) takes up the best stance possible for a bad case, namely, that the practice must be based firmly upon the Old Covenant, that it does not infuse grace of any kind but is a sign of the grace the infants may become capable of receiving at a later date. It does not appear that the diversity of covenant administration was pressed at that time, nor was it pressed a couple of centuries later when Abraham Booth wrote a three volume work on baptism. Booth like Tom Watson in our day *(Baptism not for Infants)* concentrated much on exposing the multitude of glaring inconsistencies and contradictions in the infant-baptism position and establishing at the same time a positive case with the bricks and cement of their concessions.

G. C. Berkouwer in his book *The Sacraments* traces out in usual scholarly manner the objections to infant baptism made by Karl Barth. Barth had a brilliant intellect which was quick to detect an inconsistent case. He gave non-Baptists a rough time. Rising up to meet his challenge was Oscar Cullman who laboriously put back the pieces of the Old Covenant which Barth almost succeeded in pulling down. It is only by desperately cleaving to the continuity and unity of the Covenants that their case can stand. Concentration in detail of the diversity insisted upon by the New Testament was not adequately pressed by Barth.

G. R. Beasley Murray's *Baptism in the New Testament* is a comprehensive work of great scholarship and merit. This author deals with Marcel's *The Biblical Doctrine of Infant Baptism* of which he declares that no work that he read was more unsatisfactory (p. 334). Marcel maintained that the usage and efficacy of the two rites was identical (p. 156). But Beasley Murray quotes Ernst Fuchs, 'baptism differs from circumcision as the new aeon differs from the old; the two rites belong to different worlds!' Nevertheless Beasley Murray does not attempt a detailed exposition of the difference of administration between the Old and the New Testaments.

Prof. John Murray *(Christian Baptism)* is like a defensive chess player intent on defending a position. He proceeds directly to maintain that baptism can mean something other than immersion. That is all he need to do to accommodate the 100 per cent practice of the Presbyterians to sprinkle or pour. That approach however fails to deal with the mind of the Lord on this matter. What is the mode Christ intends? With that issue Alexander Carson who was formerly a Presbyterian deals with great thoroughness and scholarship *(Baptism. Its mode and subjects)*. Also according to Prof. John Murray (to whom we owe so much on other themes), the church becomes invisible because, 'it is not the prerogative of those who administer church government to determine whether professions are true and sincere or not' (p. 41), to which absurdity we reply simply with an assertion that the business of knowing the Lord and discerning and appreciating others who know the Lord is the business of all God's people.

H. Uprichard, Joy Adams, Francis Schaeffer, Robert Rayburn, F. N. Lee and Geoffrey W. Bromiley, all contemporary authors, have written short books defending infant baptism. T. E. Watson's *Baptism not for infants* is full of quotations from non-Baptist authors showing how much they contradict each other. Paul K. Jewett's *Infant Baptism and the Covenant of Grace* consists of a positive exposition of the Baptist position as does David Kingdon's book *Children of Abraham*.